CRAFT IN THE LABORATORY

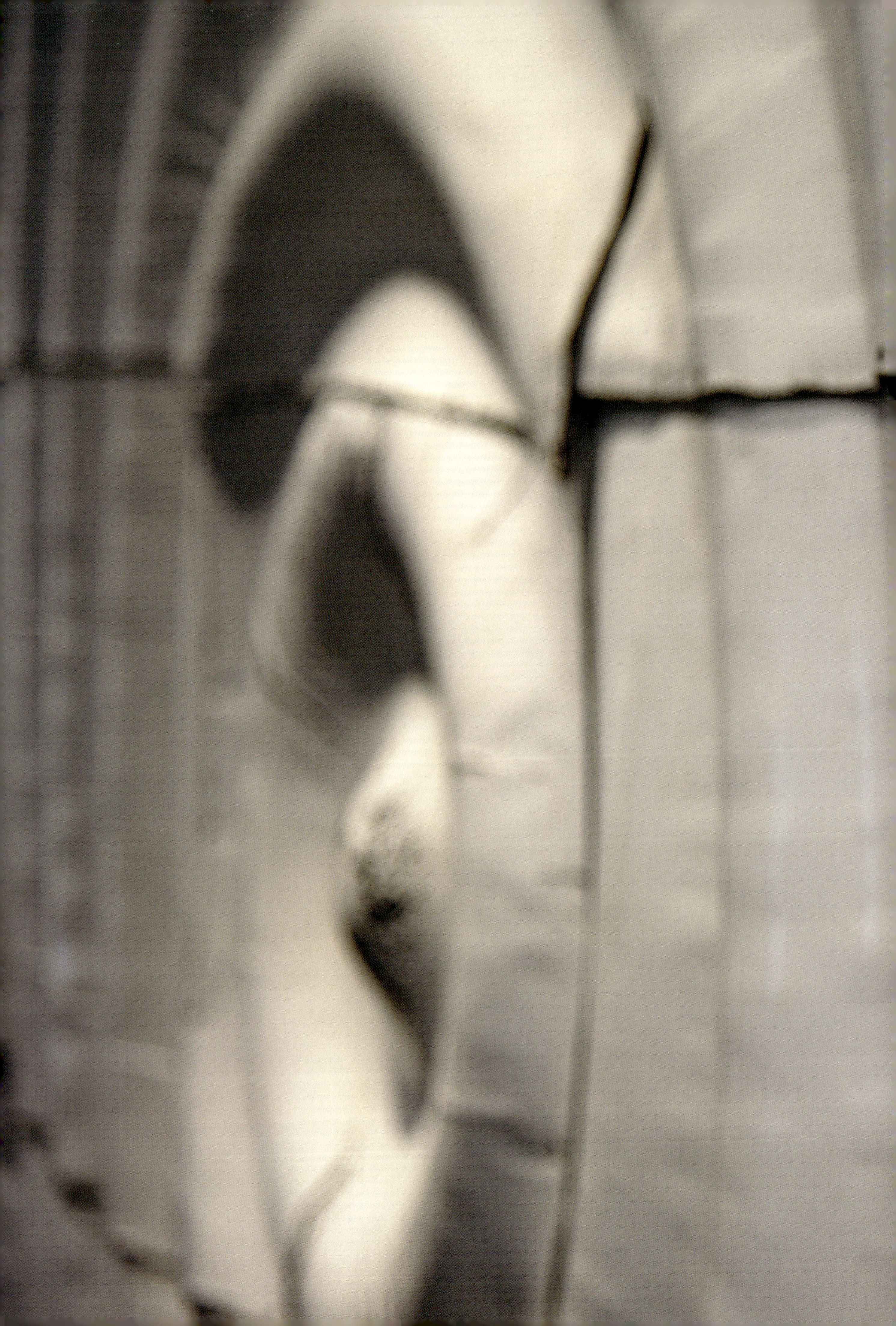

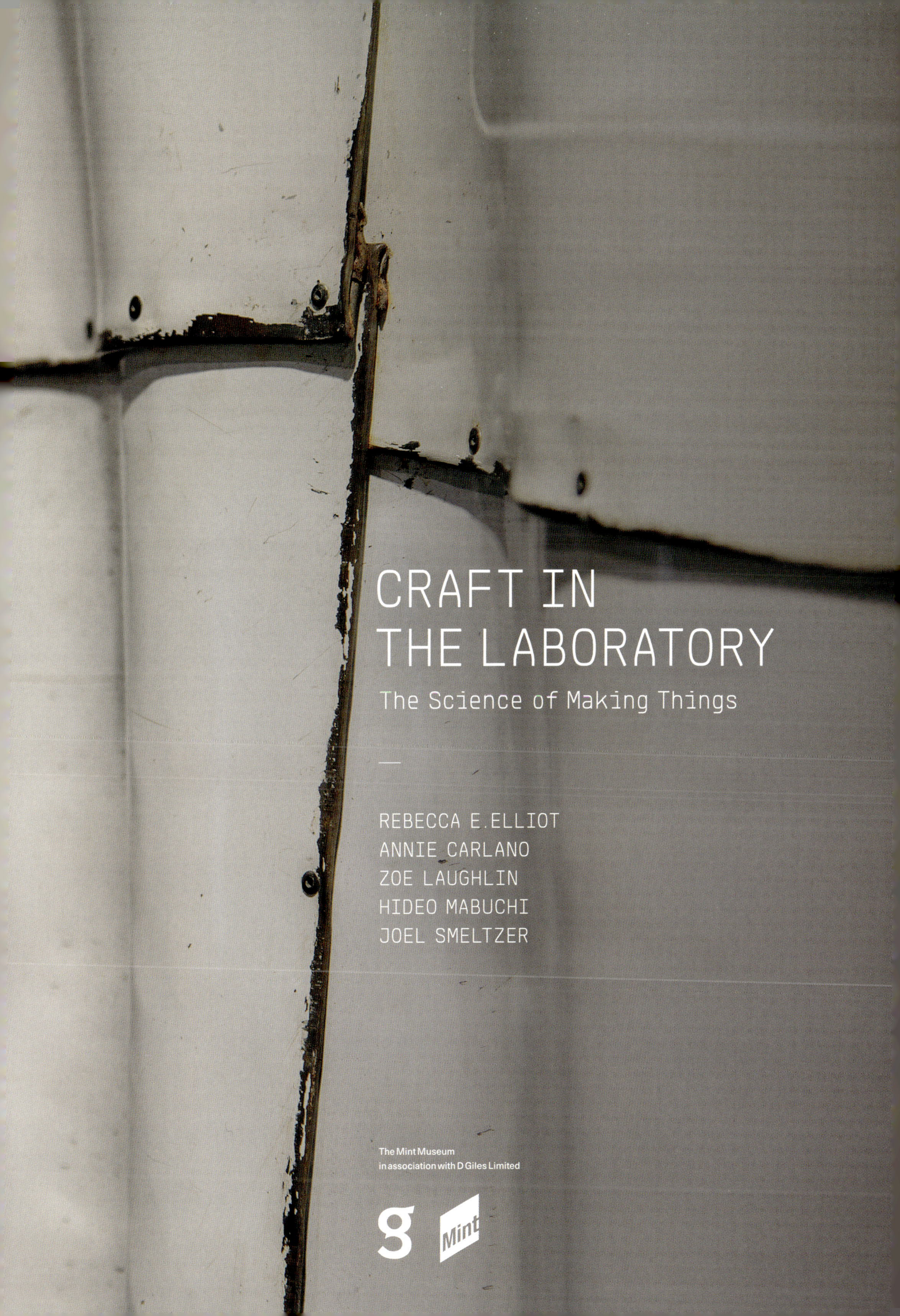

CRAFT IN THE LABORATORY

The Science of Making Things

—

REBECCA E.ELLIOT
ANNIE CARLANO
ZOE LAUGHLIN
HIDEO MABUCHI
JOEL SMELTZER

The Mint Museum
in association with D Giles Limited

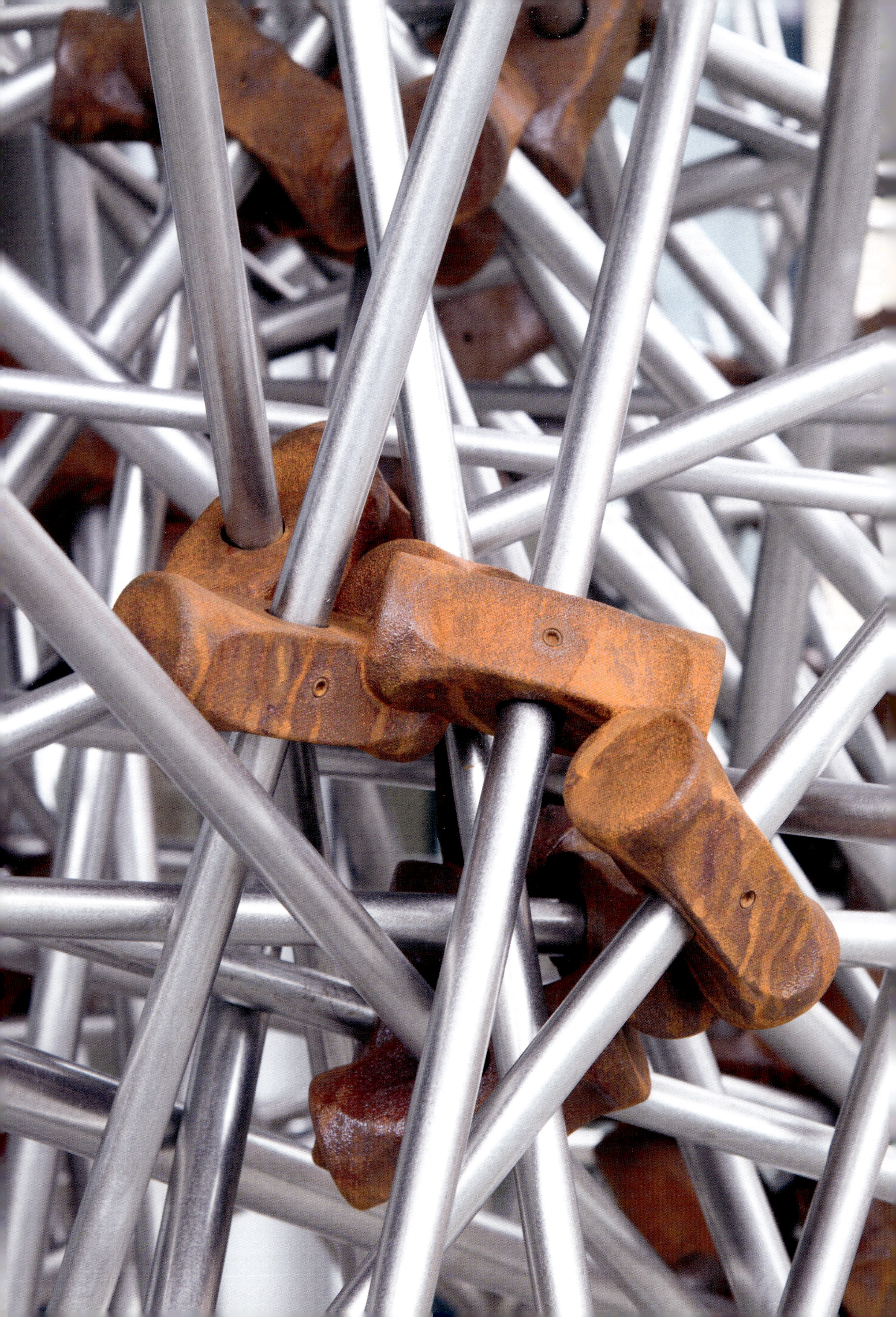

CONTENTS

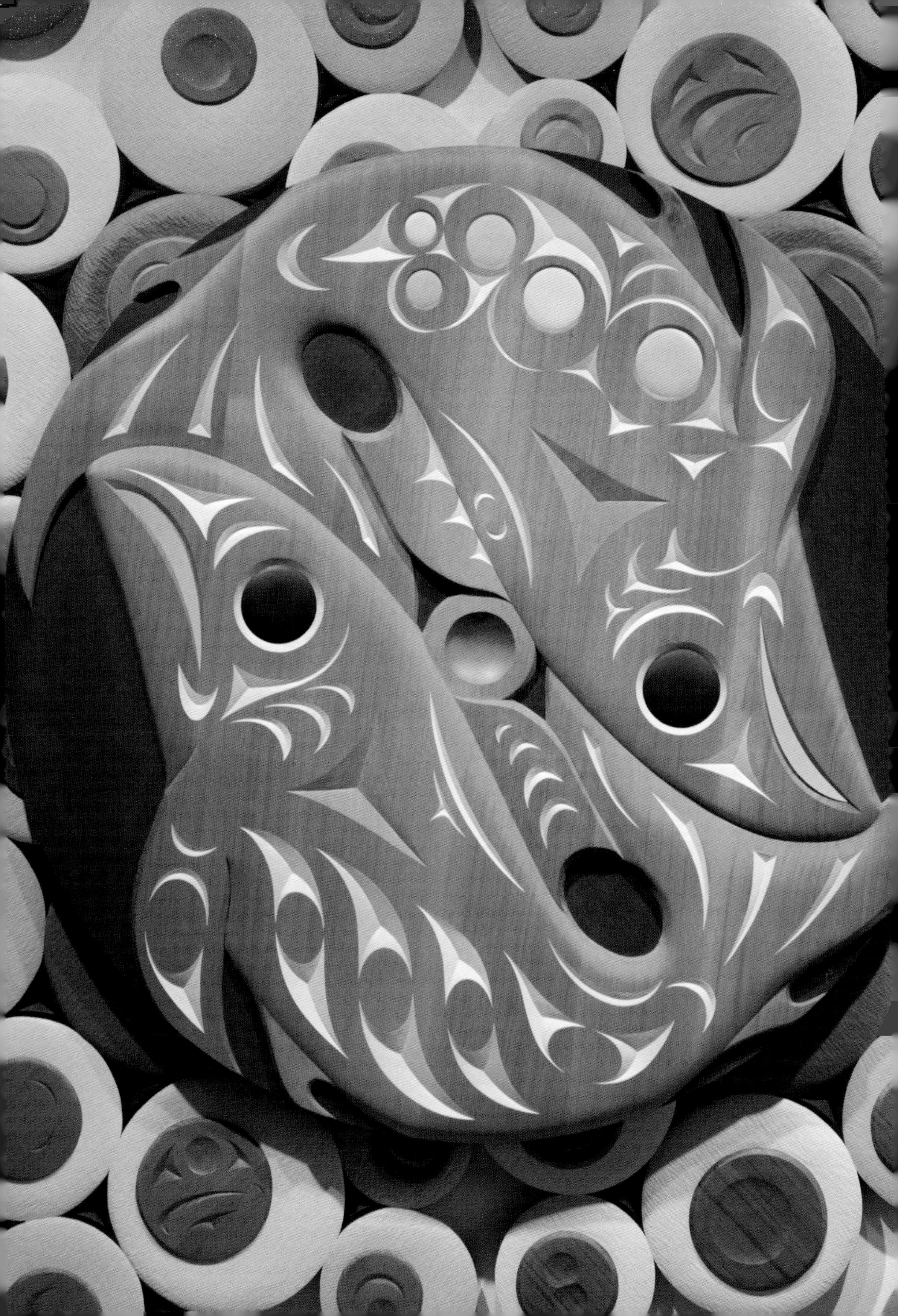

FOREWORD

Todd A.Herman, PhD
President & CEO, The Mint Museum

Even before I began my tenure as President & CEO of the Mint Museum, I was aware of the superb quality and cultural breadth of the museum's craft and design holdings. Supported by a community of collectors, patrons, gallerists, and makers, the collection has continued to develop according to stringent connoisseurship standards. Objects may carry a strong social message, or strike an emotional chord, but above all they are well designed and immaculately made. *Craft in the Laboratory: The Science of Making Things* (aka *Craft in the Lab*) presents selections from the museum's collection that exemplify how an artist's scientific thinking facilitates their making objectives. As someone who graduated with a dual major in Microbiology and Art History, I have always been keenly interested in the science behind the creation of art. *Craft in the Lab* satisfies both of these instincts and brings to the fore the incredible possibilities of a STEAM-based curriculum.

The first installation in the southeastern United States to address the subject, the theme was proposed by installation curator Rebecca Elliot, Assistant Curator of Craft, Design & Fashion, as a topic that would benefit from a collaboration with Joel Smeltzer, Head of School & Gallery Programs, who had already developed STEAM (science, technology, engineering, art, and mathematics) tours for the Mint. Annie Carlano, Senior Curator of Craft, Design & Fashion, has integrated the project into a reinstallation of the craft and design permanent collection galleries and managed the publication process. Together, they have assembled a handsome exhibition and book. Guest essayists Zoe Laughlin and Hideo Mabuchi contributed their expertise as scientists, artists, and engineers to this catalogue. We are grateful to Dan Giles and his team at D Giles Ltd. for their keen interest and sensitivity to the subject, which resulted in this beautifully designed and produced volume.

Craft in the Lab debuts as the museum celebrates the tenth anniversary of the opening of the Mint Museum Uptown; the acquisition initiative Project Ten Ten Ten; and the gift, book, and exhibition *Contemporary British Studio Ceramics: The Diane and Marc Grainer Collection*, among other milestones. It's hard to fathom how anything could surpass those multiple achievements; yet, a decade on, *Craft in the Laboratory: The Science of Making Things* breaks new ground, uniting aspects of all the above, in one exciting exploration of craft, design, and science.

The National Endowment for the Arts and the John and Robyn Horn Foundation Inc. have supported the research and publication of this catalogue. The Mint Museum is immensely grateful for the trust they have place in us and their enthusiasm for the project.

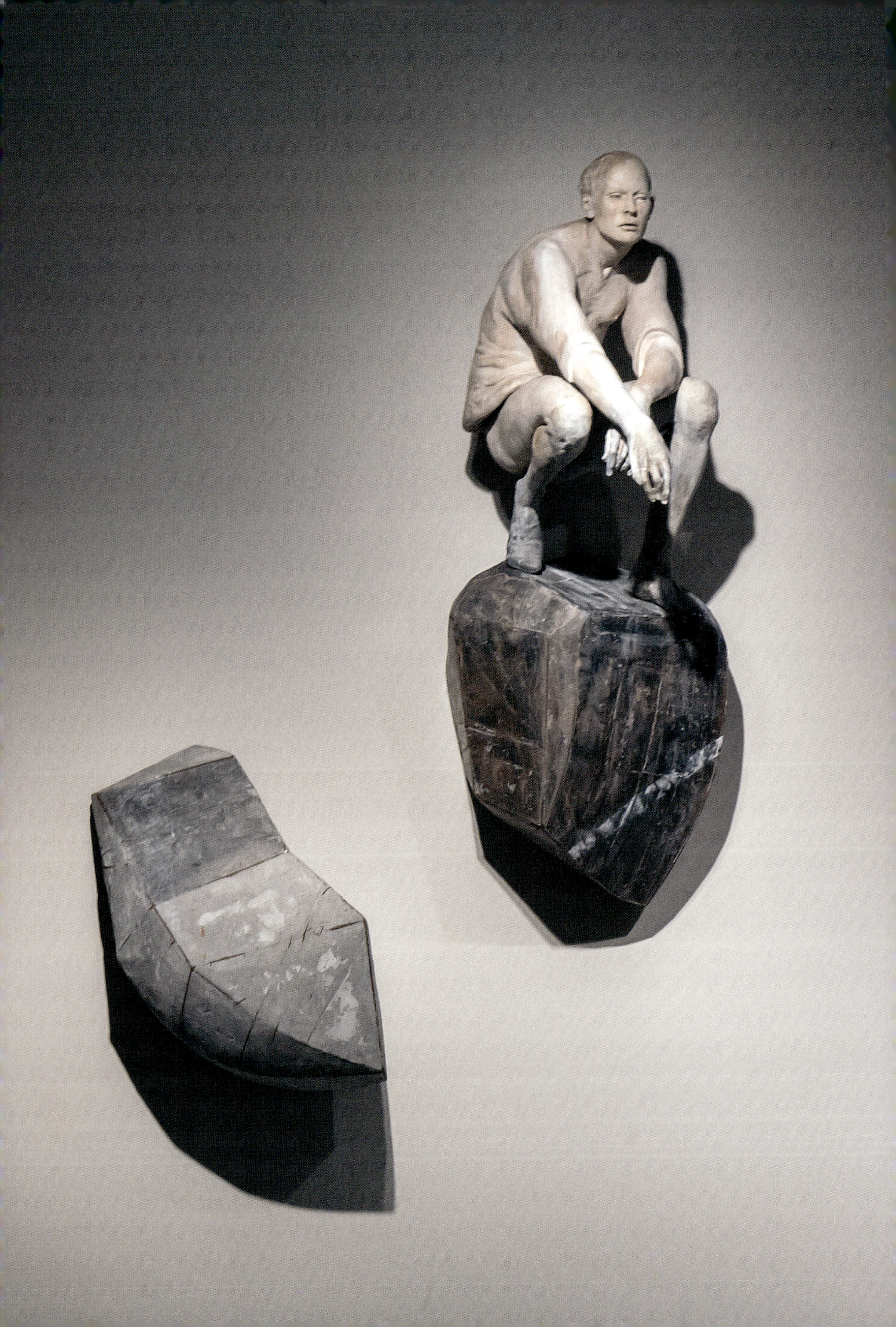

INTRODUCTION: UNDER THE MICROSCOPE

—

Annie Carlano

Since its inception in 1999, the Mint Museum of Craft + Design has focused on collecting virtuoso objects that demonstrate technical innovation and a deft handling of materials. Extending its global reach, over the past twelve years the museum has encouraged and supported even greater artistic invention, through both acquisitions and public programs. Yet, until now our installations have focused on content-driven thematic or monographic topics, selected from our permanent holdings, as well as loans from institutions, collectors, and artists. For the first time in recent history, the Mint is looking under the microscope at its own superb collection of craft and design to explore the materials and the making in greater detail, and sharing these findings through the lens of science, technology, engineering, and mathematics (STEM)—highlighting in the process the scientific inquiry that is at the core of the makers' creative process.

"WOW! Amazing! Intriguing! What is it made of? And how was it made?" In the storage room, looking at a chair or an abstract sculpture, these questions are top of mind when we, as decorative arts, craft, and design curators, examine exceptional objects. In consultation with conservators and collections managers, with surgical gloves and in lab coats, we observe wood grain, lamination processes, patina, and woven structures. In the galleries, encountering such works in wood, metal, clay, fiber, glass, or polymers, the public is eager to comprehend such things as how grains of sand become molten hot glass, and how the artist knows how much to blow, swirl, and cut.

Craft in the Lab includes highlights from the collection that put the Mint at the forefront of craft and design museums. From the inaugural gifts such as Ulla-Maija Vikman's shimmering textile hanging *11313322* (see cat. 1), to Studio Formafantasma's *Autarchy* (see cat. 5), and the most recent acquisitions including Eleanor Lakelin's *Echoes of Amphora: III/18* (see cat. 4) and Beth Cavener's *Beloved (Rearing Deer)* (see cat. 6), the criteria for collecting have focused on international contemporary works by makers that combine a reverence for and mastery of the materials with profound aesthetic and emotional impact.[1]

Perhaps no other group of objects in the collection conveys the singular artistic vision and inventiveness of contemporary makers as much as the acquisition initiative Project Ten Ten Ten.[2] Beginning with *Threshold* (see cat. 8), we experience the culmination of Danny Lane's decades-long experiments with the transformational nature of glass. In *Threshold*, as in his related architectural sculptures, Lane uses his knowledge of the science of glass and light in an undulating design in which the viewer's movements activate the experience of this sculptural wall at the entrance to the Craft + Design galleries. In the case of *Threshold*, stacked glass, seemingly laminated but in fact held in place through exacting engineering, creates a sheer prismatic veil through which we perceive color washes of the solids behind.

True lamination and kaleidoscopic color can also be seen in Patrick Norguet's *Rainbow Chair*, comprised of slices of acrylic resin, in varying acidic colors, and hand polished to make it shine (see cat 9). Intended as much as an aesthetic object as a piece of furniture, it is still produced today in the same painstaking process but in an industrial, rather than artisanal, setting.

Ayala Serfaty pursues the more poetic properties of light in *Joy of Transition* (see cat. 7). Hours of intricate lampworking are masked by a meticulous application of the polymer membrane in a cloudlike formation that hovers between two walls, the invisible craftsmanship yielding an exquisite design. Similarly, Joseph Walsh's *Enignum Motion* is an organic form whose fluid lyricism belies the many steps, from selecting the tree to heat bending the wood, and applying the lacquer, that went into its making (see cat. 11). Linked in its sensibility to both above-mentioned Project Ten Ten Ten commissioned works, and to Walsh directly through an internship in his studio, *Yumi Chair II* displays Laura Kishimoto's extraordinary skill in her own technique of free-forming bent wood (see cat. 12). Moving from the floor to the wall, *Salmon Spawning Run* (see cat. 13), by Susan Point, was created with the same sustainable making philosophy found in Walsh's work—use of local trees in their entirety—but here the elements are carved and colored with paint.

Iron is ubiquitous, plentiful in the Earth's crust, in our architecture, kitchen cabinets and offices, and inside our bodies. Tom Joyce has investigated the material for over forty years and has forged and cast iron on a monumental scale in public installations and sculptures such as *Thicket* (see cat. 14). Honoring the humble hammer, he used MRI technology to make castings of a hammer head, each then filled with filings from all his previous works and clustered to form the nuclei of *Thicket*.[3] Gold is associated with the most precious aristocratic jewelry and objects, but in the hands of Ted Noten is incorporated in irreverent, avant garde, and humorous conceptual studio jewelry, worked not at the jeweler's bench but alongside a computer. He and his assistant electroplated gold onto a 3D-printed form, embellished not with gemstones but resin daisies, to realize the surreal *Slow: Eleven Women and 400 Daisies* (see cat. 15).

So-called weeds, the plants that grow between the cracks in urban sidewalks, provided the dyestuffs for the Icelandic wool that Hildur Bjarnadóttir, together with family and friends, crocheted for her installation *Urban Color Palette, Charlotte* (see cats. 16 and 37). Setting up a dye lab in the lobby of the former Mint Museum of Craft + Design, Bjarnadóttir invited the public to participate in making the formulas, stirring the dyebaths, and setting the threads to dry. Back in Reykjavik, the yarns were hand crocheted on small hooks. Sometimes considered a weed, the bamboo plant was the material Tetsunori Kawana chose to create his ephemeral architectural

FOR THE FIRST TIME IN RECENT HISTORY, THE MINT IS LOOKING UNDER THE MICROSCOPE AT ITS OWN SUPERB COLLECTION OF CRAFT AND DESIGN.

PERHAPS NO OTHER GROUP OF OBJECTS IN THE COLLECTION CONVEYS THE SINGLE ARTISTIC VISION AND INVENTIVENESS OF CONTEMPORARY MAKERS AS MUCH AS THE ACQUISITION INITIATIVE, PROJECT TEN TEN TEN.

structure, *Passage: Waterway* (see cat. 17). Assisted by a team using simple traditional tools to split and peel the stalks, he created a structure installed for just one year, through the life cycle of the material. Seasonal climate changes to the cellulose and lignin were manifested in color fading and texture becoming dry and brittle.

Kate Malone, MBE, is inspired by the botanical world with its vibrant flowers and fecund forms (see cat. 18). Her ceramics studios both have extensive glaze "libraries," color walls displaying the results of her research into and experimentation with the chemistry of glazes. Successful firing depends on an ability to control the heat in a kiln. Decisions about kiln temperatures must be reached through a combination of mathematics and intuition. In Ben Owen III's workshop, the laboratory extends outside, where some vessels are fired in a large groundhog kiln that he (with help from others) constructed employing many engineering principles (see cat. 19). Mechanical engineering of large-scale figures and forms is an integral part of the making process of Cristina Córdova (see cat. 21). Devising armatures to support the weight of the clay is as critical to a successful outcome as the drying and firing processes.

All the makers included in *Craft in the Laboratory: The Science of Making Things* are leading practitioners in their areas of specialization. Their investigations into their chosen materials, and the way they have pushed the boundaries of what those materials can do, reflect countless hours of visionary experimentation.

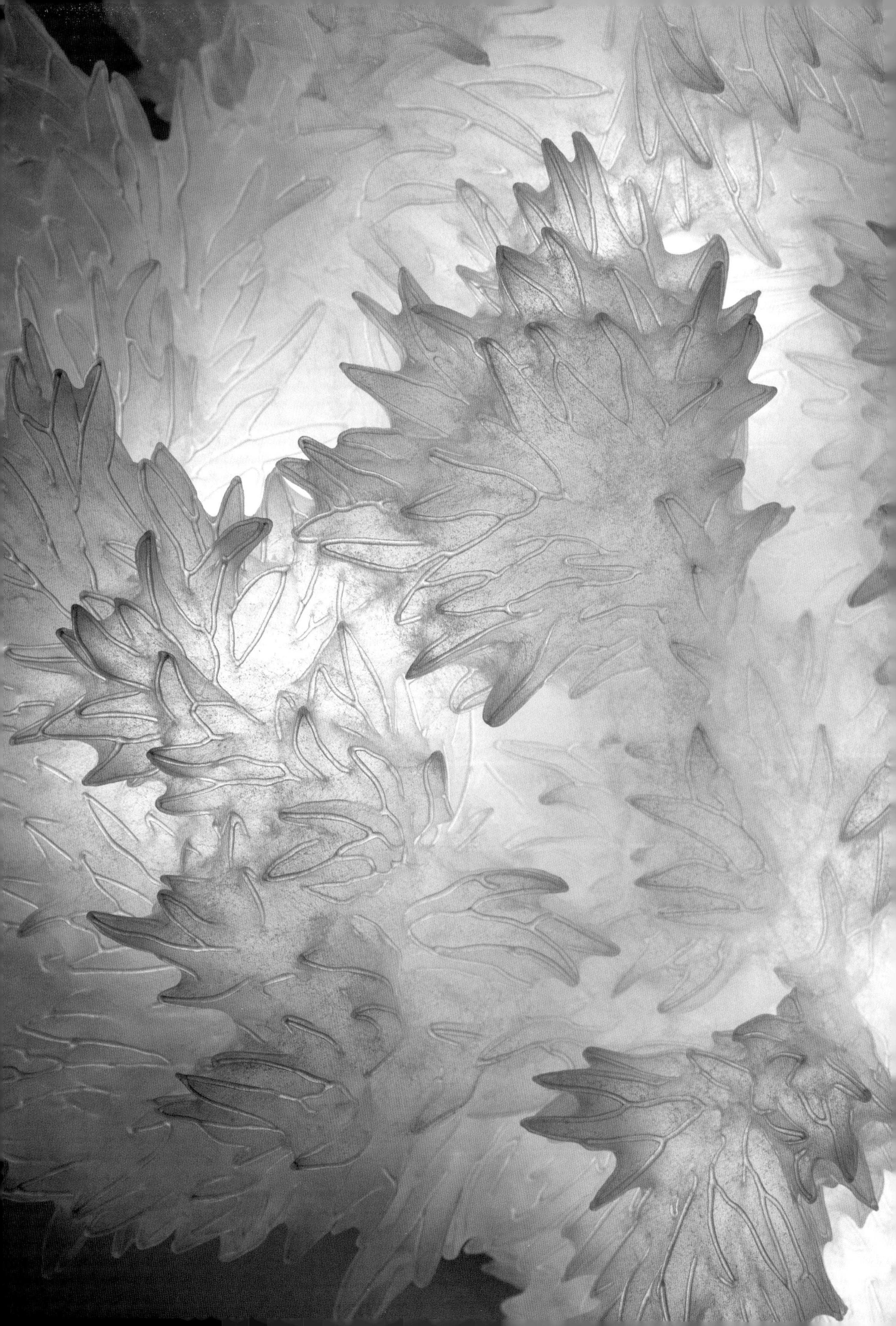

THOUGHTS ON MAKING

Zoe Laughlin

Material and process are inextricably linked. Matter is getting up to things all the time, at varying scales of time and space, in order to exist and to generate the world of objects. The process of crystallization, by which a liquid metal becomes a solid, is as important to the successful functioning of a tubular steel-framed chair as the processes of extrusion or welding are. A spectacular view across London from the 72nd-floor viewing platform of The Shard is as much to do with the subatomic structure and behavior of silica atoms that cause glass to be a transparent solid, as it is the result of the invention of the float glass process and the differing densities of molten glass on liquid tin, or the modern construction techniques employed to build extremely tall buildings. Making, in all its gloriously broad variants, is ultimately the relationship between materials and processes. The diversity of practices that are involved with, part of, and born from traditions of making—be they described as craft, engineering, architecture, chemistry, or cookery—have at their heart a shared passion for materiality, a delight in the transformative potential of stuff, and an appreciation of the potential of tools. We, the communities of makers, are bound by our shared endeavors to play with materials, to try things out and see what happens.

Making is also collaborating. There exists a strong narrative around the sciences, technology, engineering, math, and "invention" that is driven by the well-worn path of sole geniuses having solitary breakthroughs, whether it be leaping out of baths during eureka moments or toiling away in sheds to change the game for household appliances. It is far easier to write textbooks on, make television programs about, and give awards to individuals, or—at a push—small groups of people. The rules that govern the Nobel Prize, for example, clearly state a prize cannot be shared between more than three individuals. A narrative of collaboration, however, is much harder to tell. It involves lunches, walks, and talks; teachers, friends, and colleagues; love, egos, and emotions. Making anything—be that a new vaccination against an infectious disease, a range of tampons or sanitary towels that don't rely upon single-use plastics, or a contactless system of payment that works on a smartphone—requires people to work together. Innovation demands collaboration.

In an age where the dreaded acronym of STEM abounds, what does making lose? For my money it is a highly problematic label. Often linked to a dominant discourse around the particular group of subjects being the primary site of innovation, it actually fails to recognize that innovation is a function of human endeavor and, as such, no one area or group can possibly have a monopoly. If you want to know about sharpness, talk to a physicist about atomic edges, talk to a material scientist about the role of carbon in steel, consider what an experimental archaeologist working with flint has in common with a surgeon using obsidian blades, and ask a hairdresser about the effect of varying the angle of blade-attack. Better still, get them working with each other. Create a physical and conceptual space where these worlds collide, coexist, commingle, have babies and set up new and unimagined homes together. Imagine what could be made then!

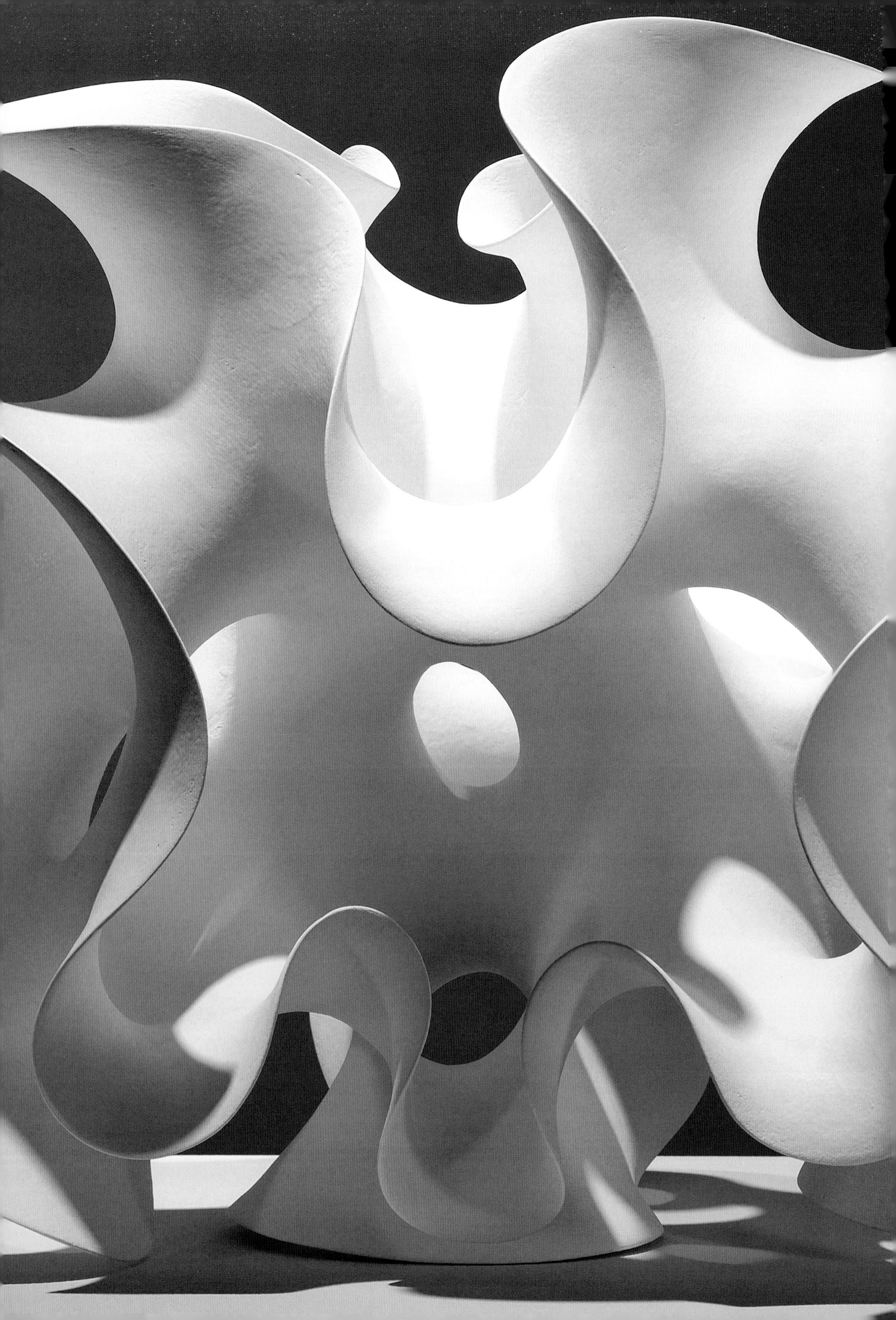

THE ART AND SCIENCE OF KNOWING THINGS

Hideo Mabuchi

I do my best not to talk shop. When asked what I do for a living I usually just offer that I'm a scientist. Sometimes I'm then asked what I study, or what kind of research I do.

Though they're probably meant interchangeably, in a way these are completely different questions—the how versus the why of focused work. I generally try to respond in some way that surreptitiously changes the subject; they're tough questions to engage in earnest, better suited to quiet contemplation than casual conversation. It's not so different from being asked what sorts of things I make, when it comes up that I craft with clay and fiber. An honest answer to that—proffered variously by many a maker—would be that I'm never really sure just what I'm aiming for, but I keep searching for clues in the studio.

Much of my laboratory's physics research over the past twenty-odd years has focused on light–matter interaction in regimes of strong mean-field nonlinearity and coherent quantum fluctuations. So I guess you could say that I study atoms and photons. As I write this I ask myself how well I feel I really know atoms or photons as a result of all this work. Not how much I know *about* them, in the way that one can know a lot about ancient Rome or about spiral galaxies, but how much I really *know* them, in the way that one knows a beloved pet or a favorite food.

Our work has utilized a single type of atom—Cesium-133, the species used in most atomic clocks. We use it because its internal structure is relatively simple and because it's relatively easy to get lasers and optics that are well matched to its particular properties. With specialized tools like tunable single-mode lasers, high-finesse micro-resonators, and feedback control systems we can make finely tailored "craft" photons that our atoms interact with especially strongly. Our experiments in recent years have studied aspects of these interactions that inform the design of novel photonic computing technologies that could offer speed and energy-efficiency advantages over conventional electronic devices.

We make photons by the septillions on an ordinary day in the lab—just by running our lasers—and they're as anonymous to me as drops in the ocean. I've never really thought to myself, *now this is a particularly nice photon*, or, *there's something a bit odd about that one*. We don't actually make any atoms—that's done mainly by stars and other nuclear reactors—but we do handle them in more intimate numbers, from wee clouds of hundreds of thousands (using optical and magnetic traps) down to singletons (using a technique called cavity quantum electrodynamics). The sophisticated experimental apparatus we build can register individual atoms and test theories about their internal dynamics, but as a conscious actor I only get to interact with atoms indirectly, through the more quotidian intermediaries that are my lab equipment. It's like interacting with the New York Stock Exchange only through the website of an online brokerage—you can probe the market's true behavior but it's nothing like being there in person. Any type of familiarity a physicist can build with atoms or photons is radically virtual, entirely mediated by rational judgments, anything but visceral.

IF ONLY WE COULD COMMUNE MORE DEEPLY WITH OUR TOOLS AND INSTRUMENTS, PERHAPS WE'D OSMOSE SOME OF THEIR MORE INTIMATE KNOWLEDGE OF THOSE ELUSIVE ATOMS AND PHOTONS.

I've burned my hand grazing a high-power laser beam, but never felt the tickle of one photon hitting my skin—our nerve receptors just aren't that sensitive. I've never pinched an atom to feel the degeneracy pressure of its electrons, never learned to tell a bosonic species from fermionic by its heft—atoms are just too minuscule. Such elementary constituents of energy and matter are imperceptible to our bodily senses; although we believe on the basis of scientific evidence that individual atoms and photons exist, they're not really entities we can ever know for real.

Thinking back over all that time spent assembling and operating complex experiments, what in fact have I best come to know? What kind of research do I actually do?

I think about soldering electrical circuits—the smell of flux and singed insulation; the heat on your face as you lean in for a closer view of what you're doing; the way molten solder wicks onto hot surfaces. I think about the way you brace two or three fingers so that you can turn a knob on an optic mount to precisely tilt a mirror without letting the weight of your hand cause wayward deflections. The feel of a twelve-point box wrench grabbing the shallow crown of a quarter-inch bolt—tenuous, yet somehow sufficient for all the strength you can muster; the hopscotch of alternately torquing this-bolt-then-that to evenly tighten a knife-edge flange against a copper gasket for an ultra-high vacuum seal. I think about pulling up a trace on an old analog oscilloscope; that ghostly glow of a phosphor screen triggered intermittently. Focusing an electron microscope—watching blurred features stretch and scrunch, hunting for sharpness with the stigmators. Tuning up a laser, any one of the many kinds we've bought or built over the past two decades, asking yourself if your alignment's getting better or worse; having to admit to yourself at 2am that you're on the wrong track.

Such manual skills and labor for such impalpable objects of study! If only we could commune more deeply with our tools and instruments, perhaps we'd osmose some of their more intimate knowledge of those elusive atoms and photons. Back in the studio I take comfort in feeling that I know my materials first-hand. It takes no effort to recall the feel of spinning clay on my fingers, or of reeling silk warp...

I think about the way my clay burnishes and cracks when I throw it dry; the way it tears as I take rough darts with a pin tool; how much water it takes to reseal the seams without leaving drips or fingerprints. When my clay hits its limit as I'm pulling it up and out, that little bit it sags as my fingers pass over it. Stacking a bisque firing, handling fragile greenware (handling other people's fragile greenware!), stilting or canting thick-bottomed pots to let out the steam; the smell of clay being force-dried in a kiln. The smell of wood-firing, the smell of reduction, the smell of too much reduction when closing up at the end of a firing; the ferocious hue of 2,400 degrees in the firebox. I think about the ache I get in my shoulders from weaving wide cloth on my floor loom, leaning over the shed with extended arms spanning a full meter to throw and catch the shuttle. The clatter of the shuttle as it jostles race and reed; the force and friction of beating picks

I'VE BECOME FASCINATED OF LATE WITH USING OPTICAL AND ELECTRON MICROSCOPES TO STUDY SURFACE DEVELOPMENT ON WOOD-FIRED CERAMICS, AND WITH THE SURPRISING CONNECTIONS ONE FINDS THEREBY TO MINERALOGY AND VOLCANOLOGY.

snug against the fell; the magic of seeing a pattern emerge in the second repeat of a long treadling sequence; the frustration of not seeing the right pattern emerge after so many hours spent threading heddles.

Studio equipment and craft processes feel so much like laboratory equipment and experimentation. In the studio, the things we make are our data. But the roles of clay and fiber seem different from those of atoms and photons; I'm not sure that knowing them is really the end. I suspect that craft materials—as central as they are to what one does as a maker—might yet be a kind of medium for some deeper investigation.

So what then would be the aim of my work in craft—what am I trying to study in the studio? My inner physicist intuits that I seek another way of knowing Nature and its habits, parallel and complementary to modern science. I've become fascinated of late with using optical and electron microscopes to study surface development on wood-fired ceramics, and with the surprising connections one finds thereby to mineralogy and volcanology. I like to think this relates to the strong focus on materiality to which I gravitate in my making—it's a story of clay leading me back to atoms and photons in a completely different context than I'd ever considered before, a much messier one that stirs a distinct sense of purpose stemming more from rapt appreciation than Baconian method.

Two centuries ago, Immanuel Kant wrote of an aesthete's urge to explore "the beautiful in nature, in order to find there, as it were, a voluptuousness for the mind in a train of thought that he can never fully unravel."[4] I wonder what animates raw materials like clay and fiber to reveal such unexpected textures as we work them. I wonder if the quantum behaviors of atoms and photons propound some cryptic new basis for building better computers. I wonder how burning wood can coax brilliant colors from drab weathered rock, and what meaning hides behind the visual resonance of wood-fired ceramic surfaces with the geological terrains clay comes from.

What are the essences of the stuff of Earth, and how can we witness their agencies? People have been exploring such trains of thought for millennia, passing down accumulated wisdom from generation to generation. Today we continue to hunt for clues in our laboratories and studios; one hardly imagines that we're anywhere near done. It's not even clear to me what kind of enlightenment we really seek, yet the will to push onward burns bright.

May we never tire in our varied practices of the art and science of knowing things.

Or of examining each other's data.

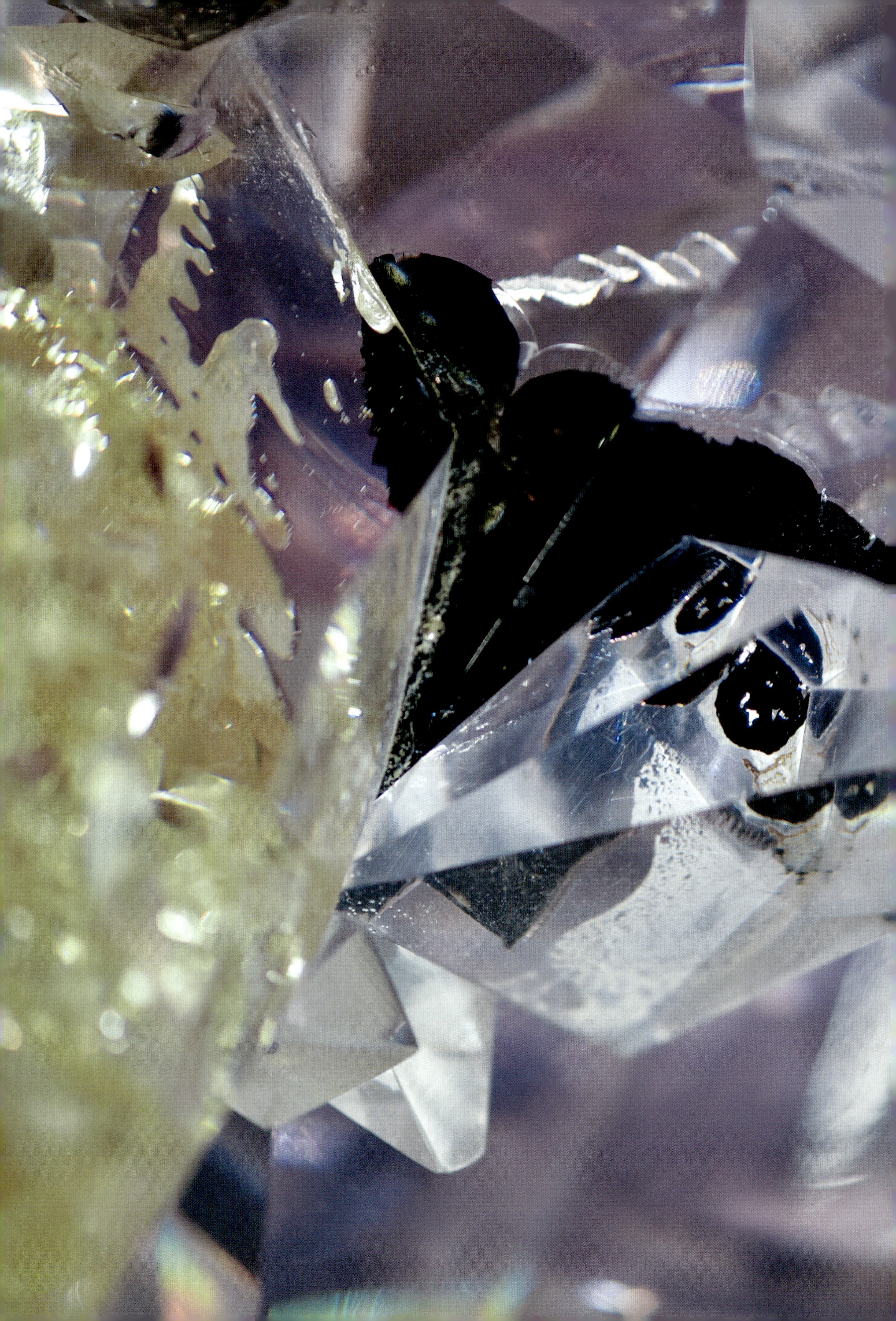

THE STUDIO AS LABORATORY

Rebecca E. Elliot

"The creative scientist needs an artistic imagination."
—Max Planck (1858–1947)[5]

Writing in the 1940s, the Nobel prizewinning quantum physicist and concert-caliber pianist Max Planck recognized something that educators, scientists, and others have rediscovered during the twenty-first century: innovation and discovery require creativity, and scientists and artists aren't so different. Fundamentally, they are both engaged in *inquiry*, "an approach to learning that involves a process of exploring the natural or material world, and that leads to asking questions, making discoveries, and testing those discoveries in the search for new understanding."[6] Research on pedagogy shows that inquiry begins with curiosity and wonder, which organically drive learners to create experiments and manipulate materials to understand phenomena. Doing science requires creative thinking; the controlled experiments and precise calculations we normally associate with science are only parts of a larger process. Making things, while it may seem playful, is also part of the inquiry process—learning by doing.[7] Ultimately, art and science are not opposites; they are simply different manifestations of inquiry.

Inverting Planck's assertion, the achievements of the artists represented in *Craft in the Laboratory* suggest that perhaps craftspeople and designers need scientific imaginations. This essay discusses a sampling of makers who have innovated within their media: blacksmiths Brent Kington and Elizabeth Brim; jeweler Douglas Harling; glass worker Paul Stankard; ceramist Takeshi Yasuda; wood workers David Ellsworth and Donald Fortescue; textile designer Christie van der Haak; and finally Ronan and Erwan Bouroullec and Tom Price, who work with polymers. Many of these makers use materials from nature that humankind has used since ancient prehistory, before science existed. The ancient people who used these materials created bodies of knowledge that enabled science to exist.[8] These makers draw from this ancient knowledge as well as scientific discoveries. They employ traditional techniques but also use inquiry to build on them and invent new ways of making. They also recognize the value of collaboration in expanding knowledge and have led their field as mentors and teachers from workshops to university level.

Sculptor-blacksmith Brent Kington and his sculpture *Weathervane* are a good place to start (fig. 1; see cat. 23). This graceful kinetic sculpture is the result of ten years spent learning blacksmithing from the ground up, in the process revitalizing the field by applying its skill set to sculpture and disseminating it throughout North America and beyond.[9] Trained in gold- and silversmithing, Kington was inspired to try blacksmithing in the mid-1960s after seeing the embellished, forged iron arms and armor at the Metropolitan Museum of Art. At the time, blacksmithing was nearly obsolete in the industrialized world, but Kington taught himself the art by consulting remaining local blacksmiths, medieval texts on metallurgy, and modern scholarship on ancient techniques.[10] By 1969, he had focused his practice almost entirely on working with iron and steel. During the 1970s, he organized three historic workshops that became known as the birth of sculptural blacksmithing, the first at Southern Illinois University at Carbondale

DOING SCIENCE REQUIRES CREATIVE THINKING; THE CONTROLLED EXPERIMENTS AND PRECISE CALCULATIONS WE NORMALLY ASSOCIATE WITH SCIENCE ARE ONLY PARTS OF A LARGER PROCESS.

(SIU), where he was a professor of metalsmithing, and the others around the southeastern United States.[11] Like Kington, attendees were mesmerized by the process of hammering red-hot metal to coax it into fluid forms. Many were professors of metalsmithing who began teaching blacksmithing in their academic programs. Kington's desire to share blacksmithing with a broader community was typical of his approach to teaching. He also helped students explore other little-known metalsmithing techniques; as former student Jan Brooks recalled, "he believed that research was a team sport ... his metals program was a vital laboratory for experimentation."[12]

Weathervane reflects Kington's own mastery of blacksmithing. Its horizontal element, terminated by discs at each end, delicately balances on the rounded point of its vertical base. With nothing but gravity holding the two pieces together, the sculpture can move in three directions, possessing pitch, roll, and yaw to sway gently in a light breeze or if touched. Part of a series that Kington made between 1978 and 1981, it evokes the weathervanes of his childhood in Kansas as well as folk-art examples seen in an exhibition at the Museum of American Folk Arts in 1968.[13] However, its fluid asymmetry and its flat discs representing the sun and moon take it beyond these precedents into the realm of modernist sculpture. Kington determined the right place for the fulcrum using intuition that surely resulted from years of working closely with metal.[14] To make *Weathervane*, Kington combined ancient forging techniques with modern ones like oxyacetylene gas welding and using a mechanical trip hammer.

Continuing this attitude of innovation, blacksmith Elizabeth Brim is known for inventing a technique to inflate hot metal into three-dimensional forms, as seen on *A Dark Tale* (fig. 2; see cat. 22). She became interested in blacksmithing while taking a jewelry class at the Penland School of Craft.[15] When given the opportunity to make her own tools in the school's blacksmithing studio, Brim was so fascinated by the process that she embarked on a career as a blacksmith, one of few women to do so in the 1980s. She soon made her name with sculptures that referenced her upbringing as a Southern woman and her interest in fairy tales, such as shoes for the Twelve Dancing Princesses. In 1992, she forged a tiara and wanted to make a pillow for it to sit on. One day, she and some artist friends were trading ideas about things they wanted to make and wondered: what if we welded two squares of steel together at the edges, left an opening for a pipe, and then blew hot air into the object? Brim tried this and it worked; the hot air inflated the steel into a pillow form that maintained its shape as it cooled. *A Dark Tale* is a later variation on the same idea.

In the field of gold- and silversmithing, inquiry often requires controlled experimentation and a precise understanding of metallurgy. To make the brooch *Vishnu Dreams* (fig. 3; see cat. 24), Douglas Harling used the ancient technique of granulation, a process he first explored as a graduate student in Brent Kington's program at SIU Carbondale in the early 1990s.[16] This demanding process entails fusing tiny spheres and wires of gold or silver onto a gold or silver surface with a eutectic bond

FIG. 1

L. Brent Kington, 1985

Myers Walker. L. Brent Kington in his workshop, 1985. L. Brent Kington papers, 1944–2012. Archives of American Art, Smithsonian Institution

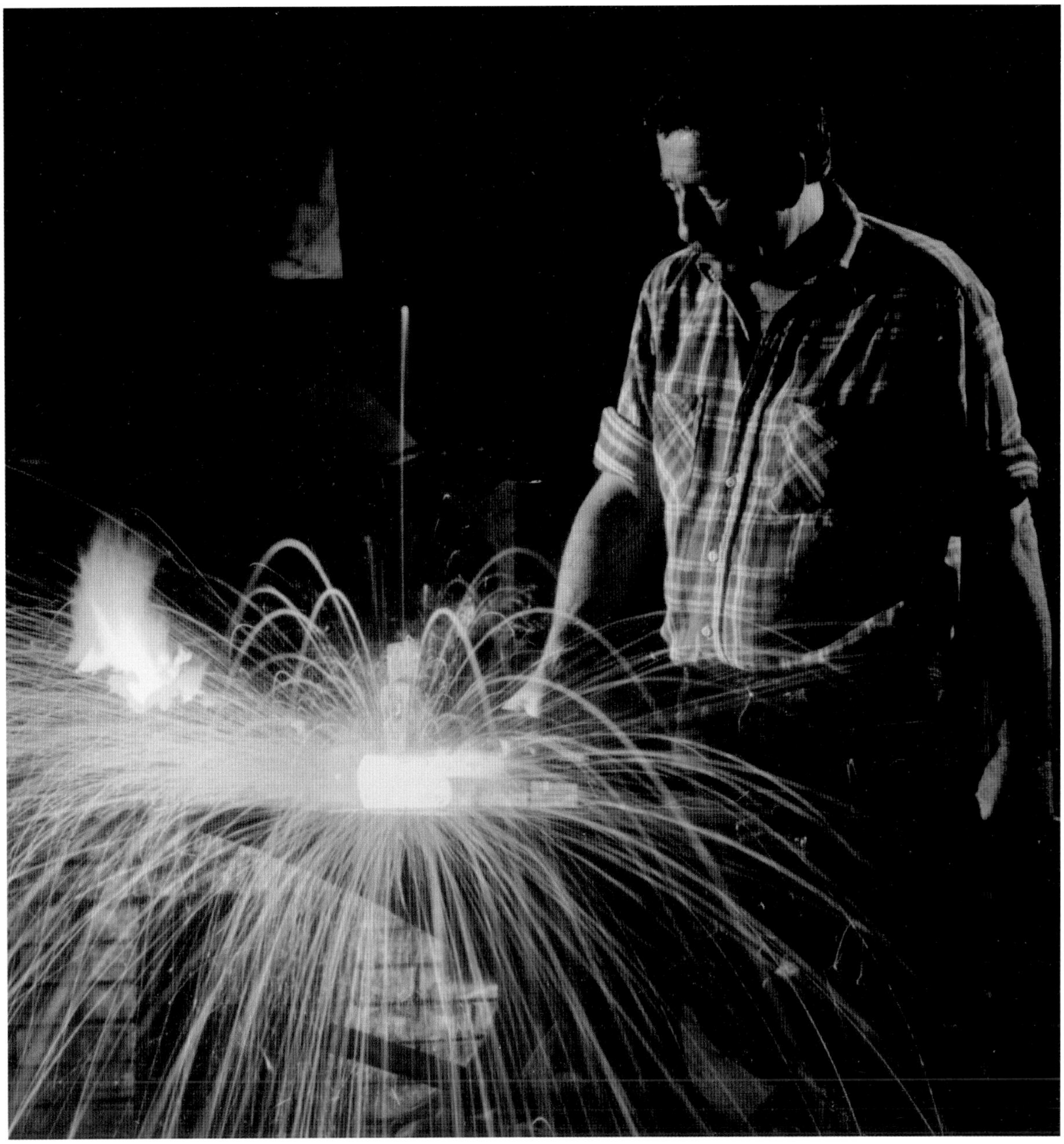

rather than solder. Harling first makes the spheres by melting bits of gold wire with a torch until they form into balls due to surface tension. Then, each gold wire or ball to be bonded is adhered to a gold surface using a mixture of animal-hide glue and copper hydroxide that also serves as a flux. He then heats the jewelry piece in a small furnace, creating an atmosphere of reduced oxygen that joins the small amount of copper in the gold with that in the copper hydroxide, forming a eutectic alloy that binds the gold surfaces to each other. Careful attention is required in applying heat: too little and the bonds do not form; too much and the gold melts. Each jeweler who practices granulation must experiment with firing time and temperature to find the right combination. The imagery of *Vishnu Dreams* suggests Harling's affinity for scientific thinking: the sugilite stone reminded him of the photos of retinas that his ophthalmologist father used, suggesting the mind's eye and fitting Harling's theme of the Hindu tale of Vishnu dreaming the universe into existence.

Paul Stankard's path of inquiry led him from working as a scientific glassblower to making floral paperweights and ultimately to reinventing this format to create intricate glass sculptures like *Carolina Bouquet Botanical* (fig. 4; see cat. 25). He spent the 1960s working as a scientific glassblower, using a torch to form borosilicate glass into complex apparatuses used in scientific experiments.[17] The existence of this vocation highlights another link between craft and science:

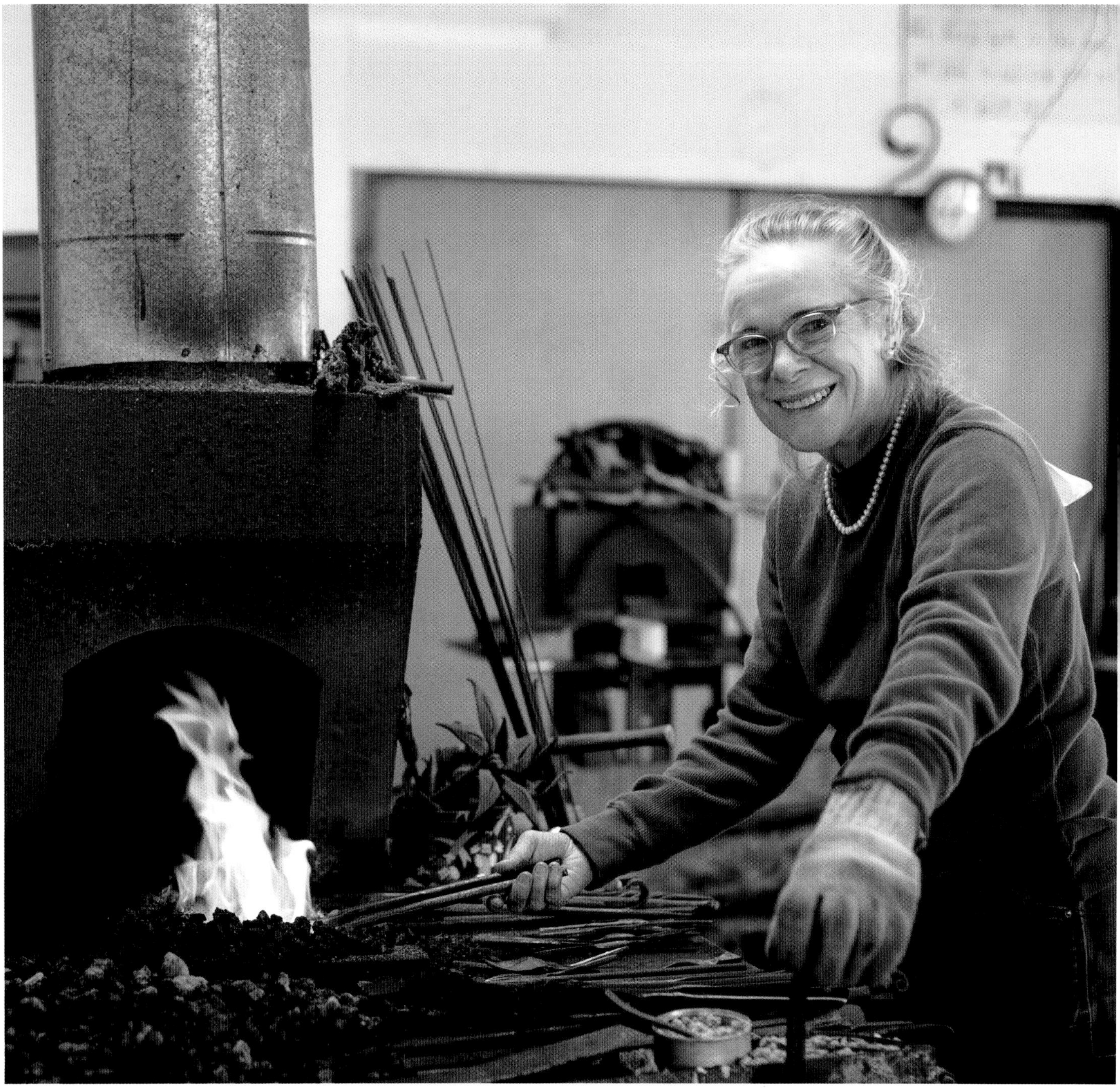

craft skills have long helped make scientific discoveries possible.[18] In the late 1960s, seeking a creative outlet, Stankard began teaching himself to lampwork floral paperweights, a longstanding tradition in New Jersey, but one where the few remaining makers kept their techniques secret. This craft involves using a torch to heat colored glass rods and form them into flowers, then carefully dropping a gather of hot, clear glass over the flowers to encase them.

By 1972, making paperweights became Stankard's full-time job, and over the following decades his skills continued to grow. Flowers became more and more realistic (even when they were his own inventions), and glass leaves, insects, soil, and roots were added to create microcosms of nature. In 1980, he developed the Botanical format, in which the clusters of plants above ground are mirrored by root systems below ground, with each half made separately, encased in its own gather of clear glass, joined, and annealed as one. The process is precarious; as late as 1988, each lampworked cluster could take up to three days to create, and the overall failure rate for these sculptures was 30 percent.[19] Nonetheless, Stankard's work has only grown

FIG. 2
Elizabeth Brim
Courtesy Elizabeth Brim.
Photo: Nick King

IN THE FIELD OF GOLD- AND SILVERSMITHING, INQUIRY OFTEN REQUIRES CONTROLLED EXPERIMENTATION AND A PRECISE UNDERSTANDING OF METALLURGY.

more complex, later incorporating lampworked supernatural "root people" and cast glass masks, as seen in *Carolina Bouquet Botanical*. Stankard has also shared his skills broadly by teaching at his community college alma mater and at workshops all over the country.

Unlike glass or hot metal, clay can be handled directly by the artist. Takeshi Yasuda's career has been a lifelong conversation and ongoing experiment with clay and gravity, resulting in unusual forms like *Qingbai Celadon Bowl with Golden Interior* (see cat. 26). Trained as a potter in Mashiko, Japan, he is a master of throwing on the wheel, which requires total focus and control over a spinning glob of wet clay. As Yasuda says, "You have to become aware of the centrifugal force and then ... work against it, or ... work with it."[20] Eventually, Yasuda started thinking about the other force affecting the clay—gravity—and began allowing it to help create his forms. *Qingbai Celadon Bowl* is made of porcelain, the clay body that is the thinnest, wettest, and arguably the most difficult to handle. Yasuda first threw a large, shallow bowl on the wheel, allowing the impressions of his fingertips to remain. Then, raising the bowl (still stuck to a circular board called a bat) above his head, he lowered it towards the floor without letting go, shedding a ring of clay from the top and creating the bowl's irregular rim (fig. 5). He modified the form further by using his palm to push on the vessel's walls from the inside, creating raised areas.[21] After bisque firing, the bowl received glazes that combine tradition with innovation. Its exterior was glazed with a traditional Chinese celadon glaze whose color comes from a trace amount of iron in silica. The interior is glazed with colloidal gold, its superlative shine derived from highly reflective gold nanoparticles.[22]

Artists who specialize in wood or fibers contend with the idiosyncrasies of materials that were once living. David Ellsworth has become known for expanding the possibilities of lathe-turning wood by developing the technique of blind turning to make thin-walled vessels with

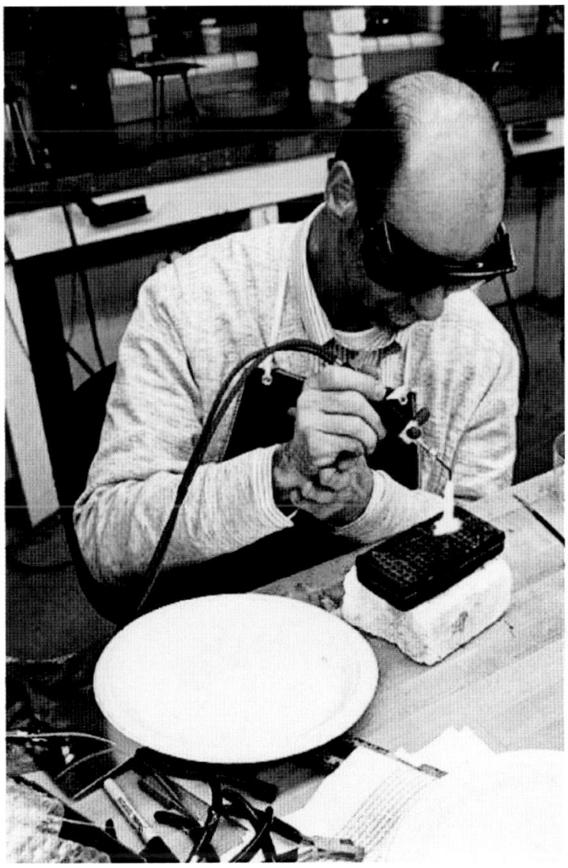

FIG. 3
Douglas Harling
Courtesy Douglas Harling

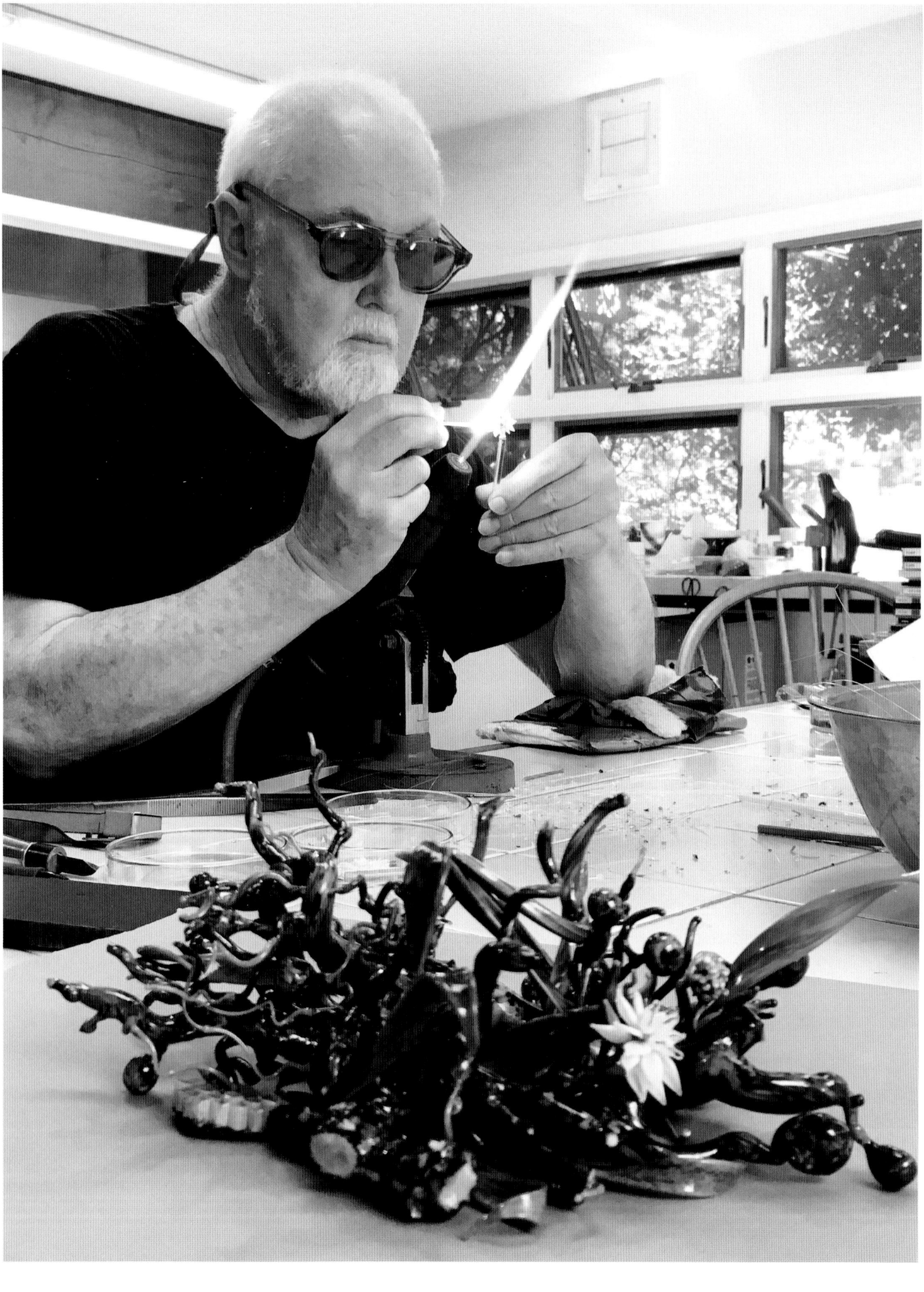

THE DESIGNERS, ARTISTS, AND CRAFTSPEOPLE DISCUSSED HERE REPRESENT JUST A FEW OF THE INFINITE WAYS THAT MAKERS USE THE INQUIRY PROCESS TO MAKE REMARKABLE WORKS OF ART AND DESIGN.

very small openings, often using wood afflicted by diseases that changed its grain and made it difficult to turn (fig. 6). Trained as a sculptor, Ellsworth's education included working with clay, and his wood vessels are influenced by Toshiko Takaezu's work as well as southwestern Native American pots, particularly those of Hopi potter Nampeyo (1859–1942), whose olla pots the shape of *Untitled Vessel* resembles (see cat. 27).[23] He does not simply impose his compositional ideas on the wood, however; rather than design pieces beforehand, he determines forms by responding to the wood's characteristics. *Untitled Vessel* is made from spalted beech, its dark lines created by a fungus. Ellsworth oriented it on the lathe so that turning it produced wing-like shapes wrapping from its opening around its sides. He also preserved evidence of the wood's origin as part of the tree, incorporating both heartwood and sapwood, and leaving areas of bark. To hollow the inside of *Untitled Vessel*, he used a bent metal chisel he invented in 1976 that requires the woodworker to cut away wood without the benefit of sight, hence the term "blind turning." The technique requires an understanding of, and sensitivity to, the texture and structure of the wood.

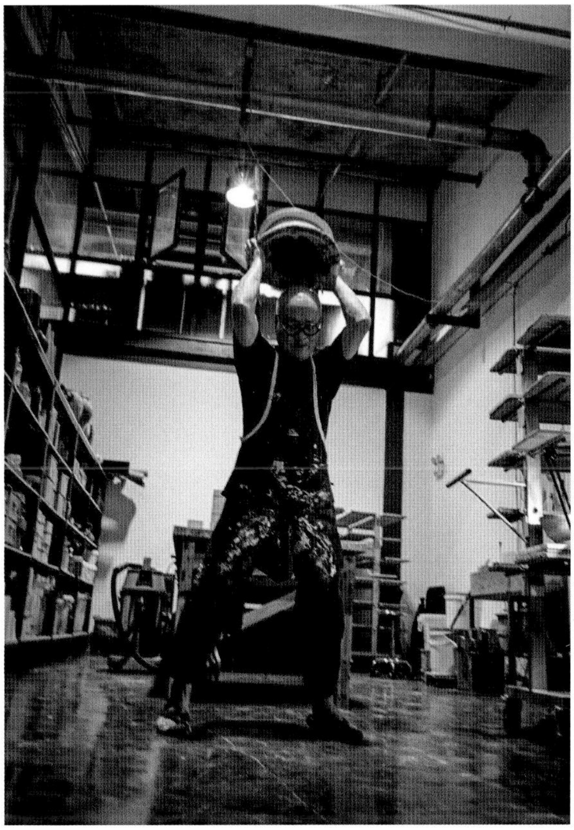

FIG. 4
Paul Stankard
Courtesy Paul Stankard

FIG. 5
Takeshi Yasuda
Courtesy Takeshi Yasuda
Photo: Min ZHAO

Donald Fortescue takes a contrasting approach to creating lathe-turned wood sculptures like *Pike Basking* (see cat. 28). He constructed it from rings of laminated birch plywood whose measurements he calculated beforehand on paper, which an assistant cut out. Fortescue then glued the rings into sections based on a precise technical drawing he had made, turned them on a lathe to refine their shape, and finally assembled, sanded, and polished the sculpture. He finds the creative process most satisfying when he works within parameters that he sets before he starts making. He also prefers materials that give him a high degree of control. Usually, wood turners and furniture makers must work around the grain and idiosyncrasies of wood, as well as its ability to expand and contract with changes in humidity. In laminated plywood, the grain of each layer runs perpendicular to the last, making grain irrelevant as a design factor. And using a system of smaller

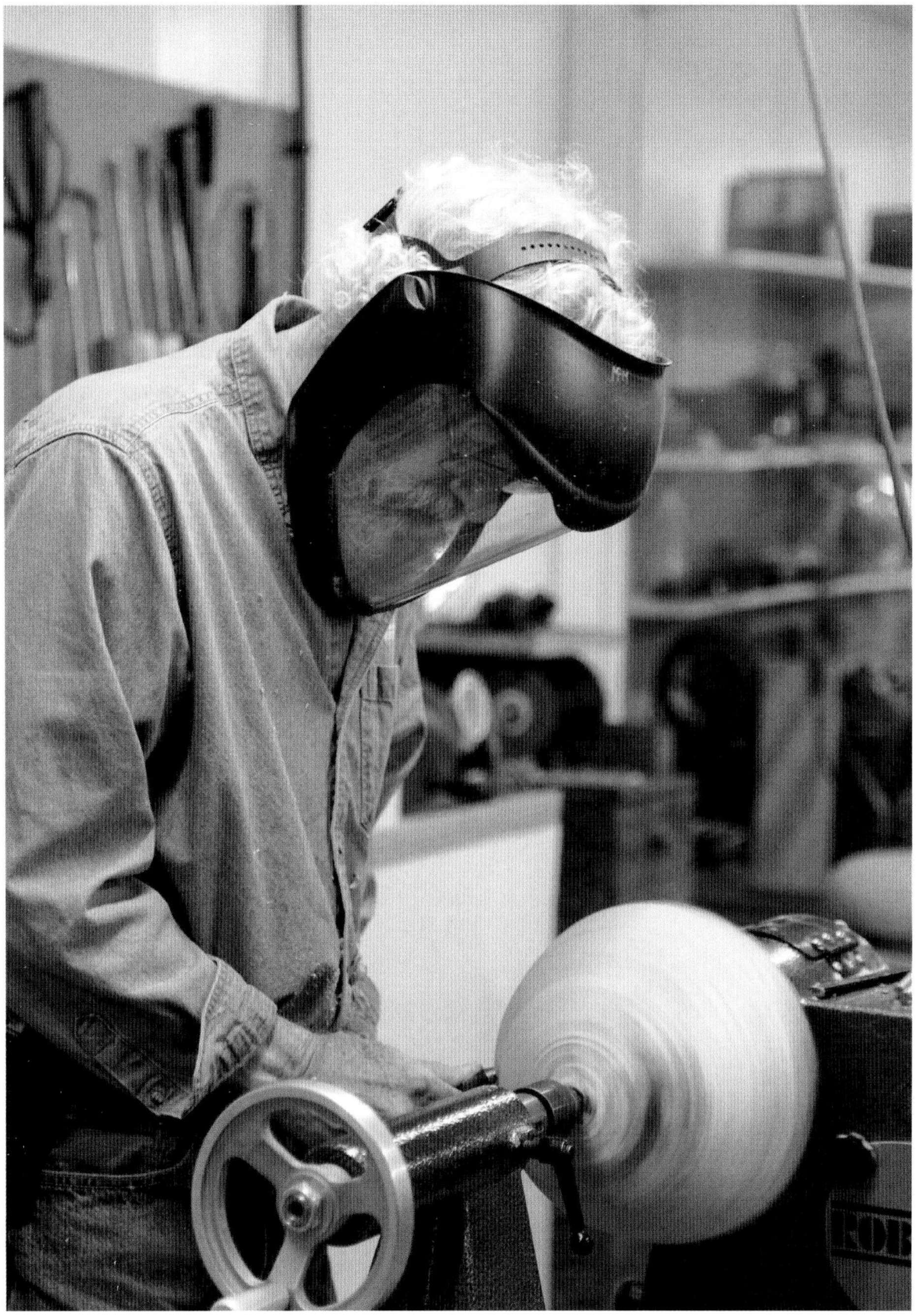

FIG. 6
David Ellsworth, 2019
Photo: Gennifer Stanley

units to create *Pike Basking* and other sculptures allowed Fortescue to make any form he could imagine, unlimited by the size of a piece of wood. At the same time, it allowed him to deviate from his plan: originally *Pike Basking* was to have two tapered ends that curved towards each other, but in assembling it he chose to make each end curve the opposite way, rendering the sculpture more zoomorphic and dynamic.[24]

Fortescue thinks about wood like a scientist or an engineer, which is not surprising considering his training. He earned a BS in botany from the University of Sydney (1979) and worked as a researcher and botanical illustrator in that field before becoming interested in woodworking. His additional degrees include a diploma for design in wood from Australian National University (1987), a master's degree in sculpture from the University of Wollongong (1995), and, most recently, a PhD in sculpture from Australian National University (2019). Fortescue has a lifelong interest in science, and after making *Pike Basking* his work evolved to address themes of scientific discovery through installations and site-specific sculptures that include wood but are not primarily made from it. His most recent work relates to his artist residencies working alongside physicists at the north and south poles.[25]

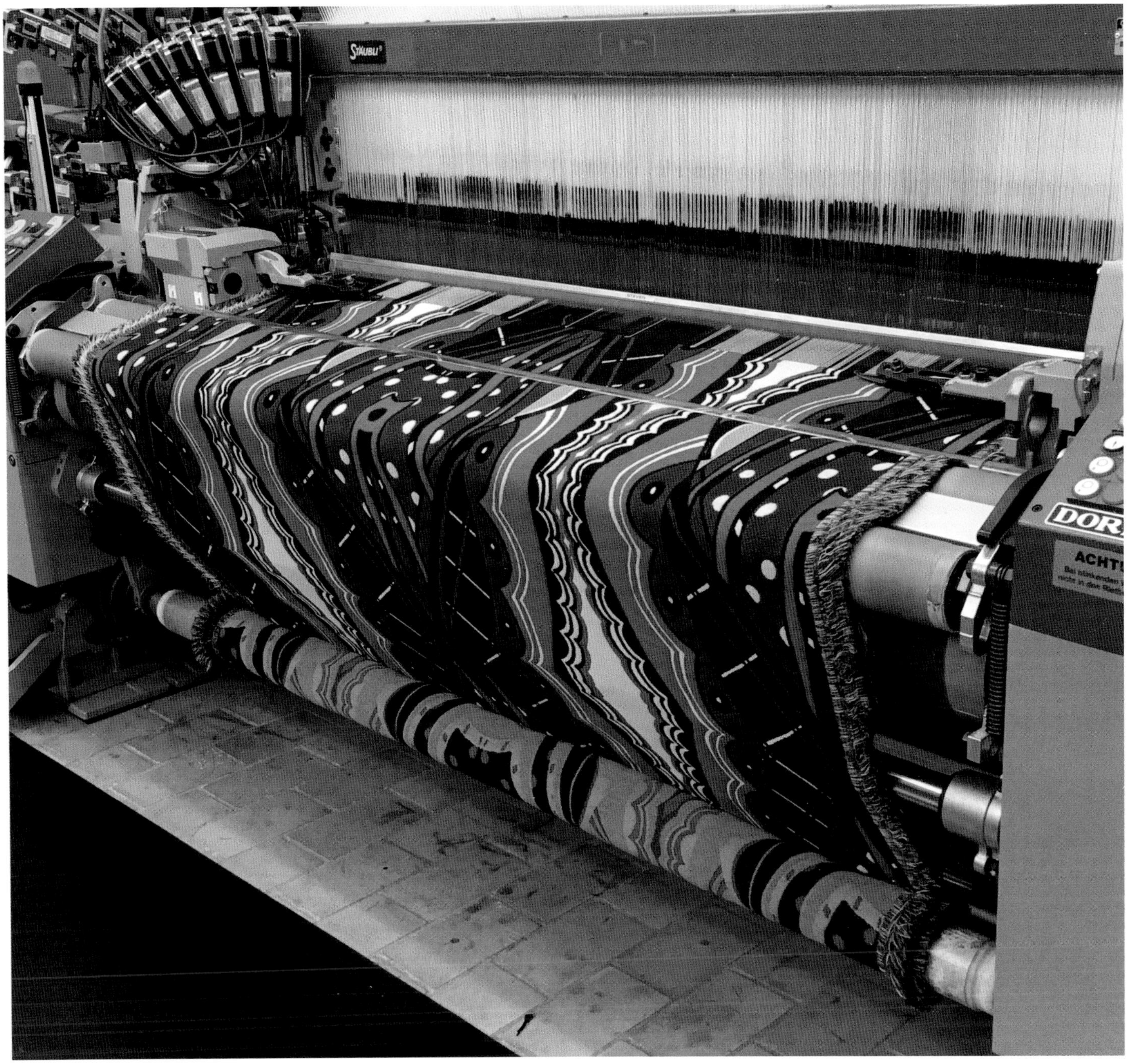

FIG.7
Edda on the loom, TextielLab at the Textile Museum, Tilburg
Courtesy Christie van der Haak

Christie van der Haak works in a looser, more spontaneous way to explore pattern and color through woven textiles. To create *Edda*, she first designed an abstract motif on paper with felt-tip pen and gouache, looking at the motif with a mirror while she designed it to visualize its symmetrical repeat (see cat. 30).[26] Van der Haak worked with technicians at the TextielLab of the Textile Museum in Tilburg, the Netherlands, to transform her design into a computer program that controls the Jacquard loom that wove the textile (fig. 7). The advanced, computer-controlled looms at the TextielLab can produce endless multiples of the same design, but, paradoxically, they also allow artist-designers like van der Haak to create unique works by making spur-of-the-moment decisions. Van der Haak can stand at the loom as a design is being woven and tell the technicians to stop the loom, change the threads or yarns to a different color scheme, and continue weaving. This process allows her to paint with the loom, which appeals to van der Haak as an artist who created complex, richly patterned, colorful paintings for many years before turning to textile design in 2003. Although she did not make such changes on *Edda*, she has used this approach to create lengths of patterned upholstery fabric—an example of the mass customization that has

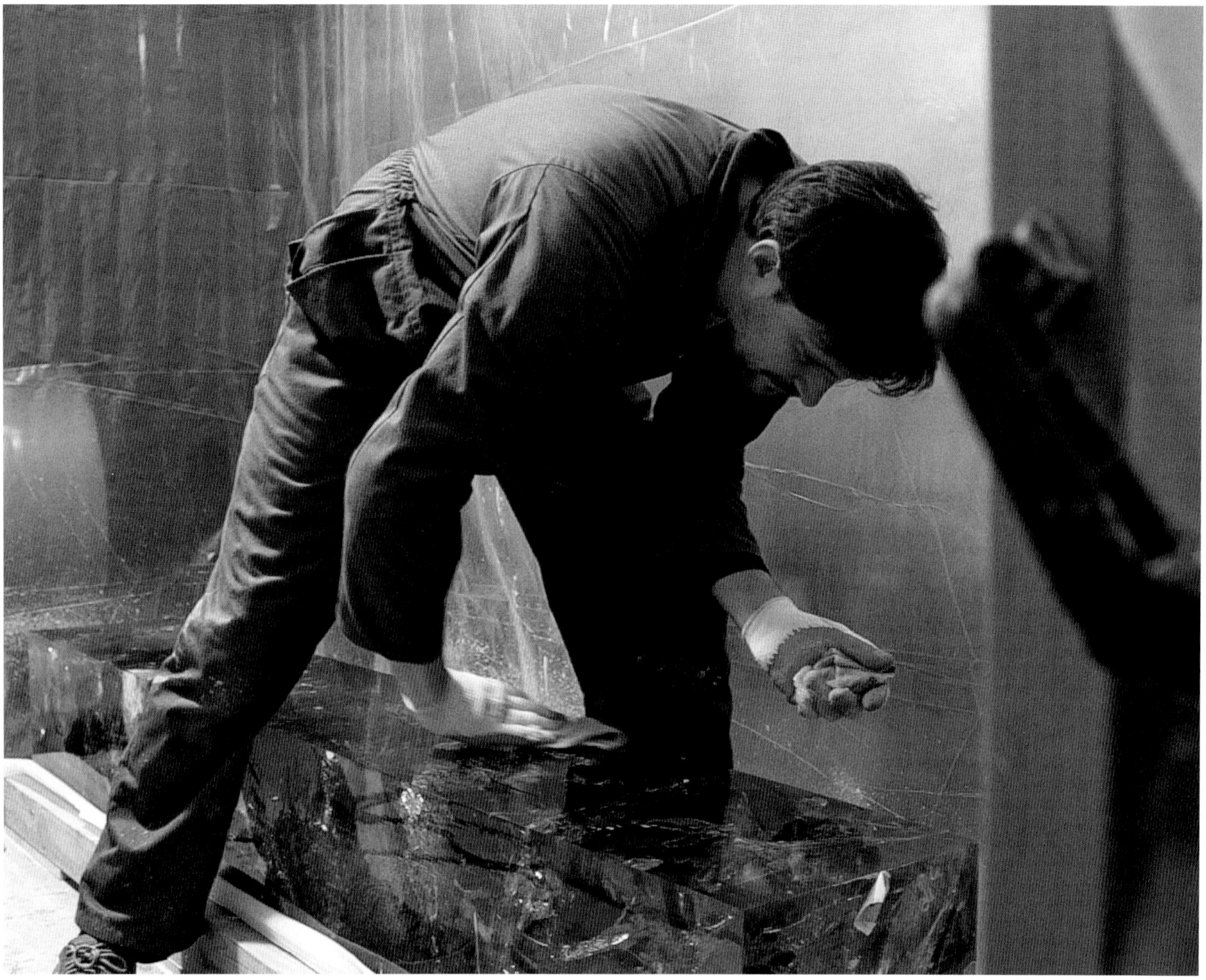

become possible through advanced production technology in twenty-first-century design. It is also an example of the many kinds of experimentation with textiles that take place at the TextielLab, founded in 2005 and re-envisioned in 2013 as a place for artists and designers to test ideas by working with technicians.[27]

The experience of brothers and designers Ronan and Erwan Bouroullec in developing the injection-molded plastic *Vegetal Chair* for Vitra shows that the same process of inquiry and experimentation can occur even within the economic and technical limitations of mass production (see cat. 29). The *Vegetal Chair* grew out of the Bouroullecs' and Vitra's successful collaboration on *Algues* (2004), a modular system of plastic branching forms that users could connect into room dividers. The Bouroullecs wanted to design a chair that, like *Algues*, was inspired by growth patterns in nature. From the outset, they and the product development team at Vitra knew that durability, affordability, and the complexity of the design concept required the chair to be injection-molded in plastic.[28] The challenge was to harmonize the design with the capabilities of the technology and the material. In this process, hot, liquid plastic is injected into a mold at high pressure and must flow evenly into all parts of the mold before it cools, solidifies, and is removed, all in less than two minutes.[29] The designers worked with Vitra for nearly four years to arrive at the final design. Their process was at once artisanal and high-tech, involving handmade drawings on paper and hand-carved scale models, but also virtual modeling software and CAD-produced prototypes. Ultimately, the final design simplified and abstracted the Bouroullecs' initial concept into a motif of asymmetrical,

FIG. 8
Tom Price
Courtesy Tom Price

ARTISTS WHO SPECIALIZE IN WOOD OR FIBERS CONTEND WITH THE IDIOSYNCRASIES OF MATERIALS THAT WERE ONCE LIVING.

geometric, branching openwork on an elegant, versatile, award-winning chair.[30]

We usually associate plastic with industrial production, but Tom Price, creator of *Synthesis X*, has explored a variety of polymer types in his studio to create furniture, lighting, and sculptures (fig. 8; see cat. 31). Price holds degrees in sculpture as well as furniture design; his practice exists somewhere between the two and is rooted in his curiosity about materials.[31] These range from polypropylene and polyvinyl chloride to, in the case of the *Synthesis* series, resin and tar. Rather than begin with a plan or a drawing, he gets ideas from materials and the way chance events act upon them. *Synthesis* is a series of illuminated sculptures whose crystalline appearance results from injecting tar into resin as it cools. Price knew that fissures and cracks form in resin when it is mixed incorrectly and exploited this feature by experimenting with the proportions of resin and catalyst.[32] Finding the petal-like cracks too conventionally pretty, he sought another substance to react with the resin. He chose tar because he liked the way this solid, black substance contrasts with clear, liquid resin. As the resin cools and solidifies, fissures form and an exothermic reaction occurs, causing the tar to melt, expand, and force its way into them. This creates dramatic internal formations and colors, ranging from pinks and purples to gold, green, brown, and black. Each *Synthesis* sculpture is unique, and Price has little idea what the blocks of resin will look like until they are released from the mold in which the chemical reaction takes place. *Synthesis X* was assembled from blocks of resin that were cut in geometric shapes and polished. More than an interesting technical feat, the process of *Synthesis* also has metaphorical meaning for Price; he considers it "the study of a dialogue between two contrasting materials ... and their negotiation for space and identity when forced to become a single unified entity."[33]

The designers, artists, and craftspeople discussed here represent just a few of the infinite ways that makers use the inquiry process to produce remarkable works of art and design. They show us that art and science ultimately spring from a common well of human curiosity. At a time when science literacy is more important than ever, they help us see what it really means to think like a scientist. It means exploring the world, asking questions, trying out ideas, playing with materials, and *making things.*

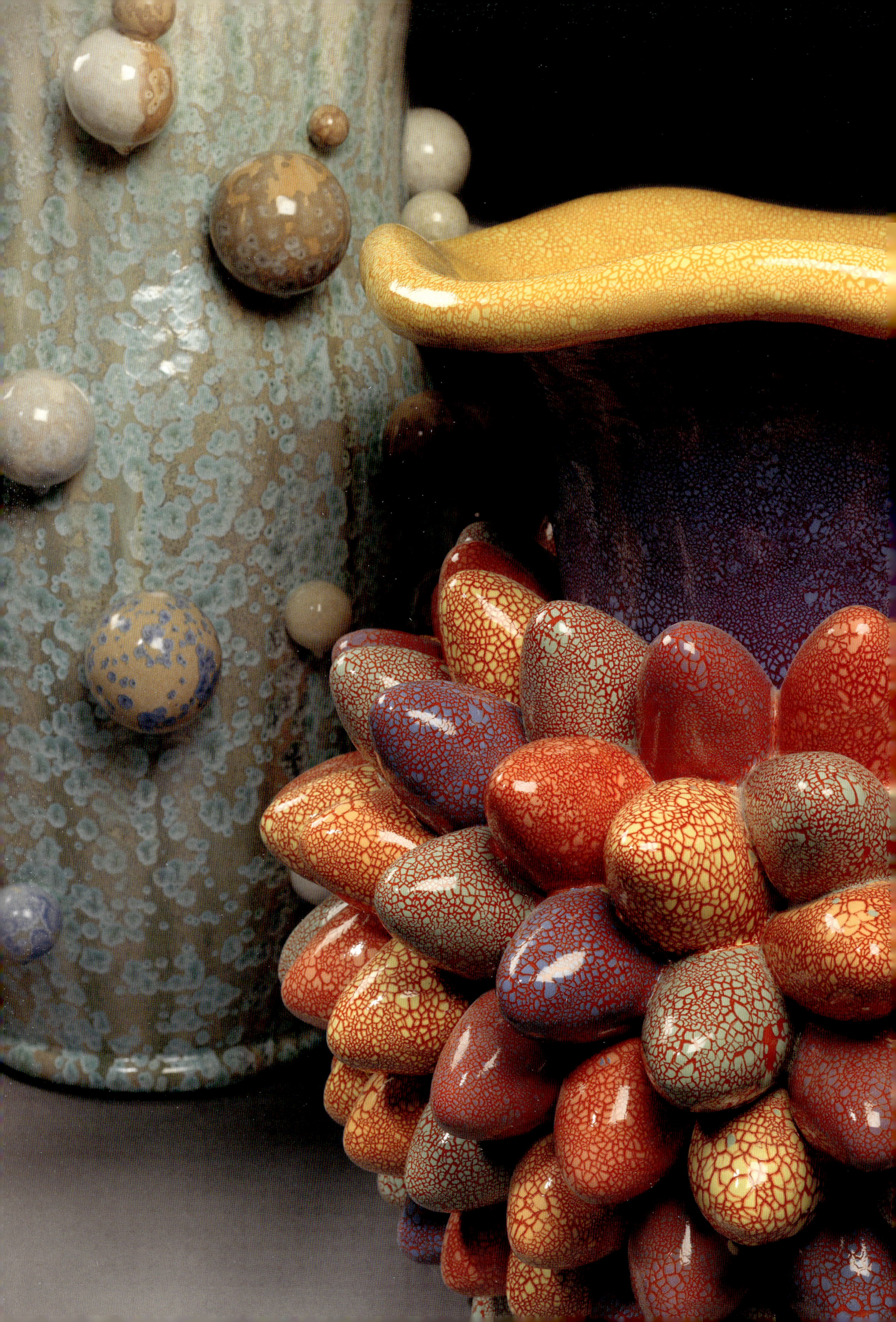

OBSERVATIONS

Joel Smeltzer

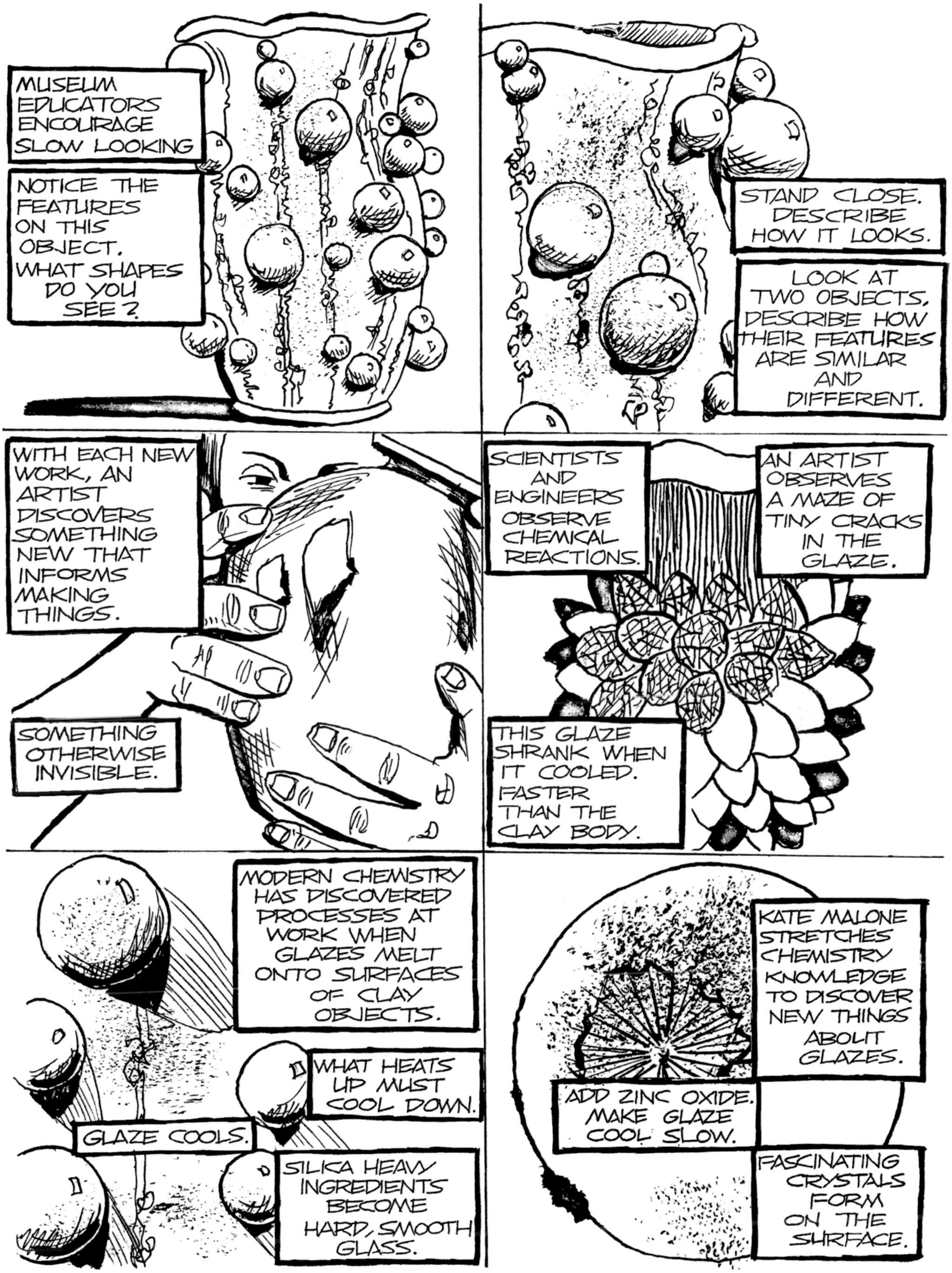

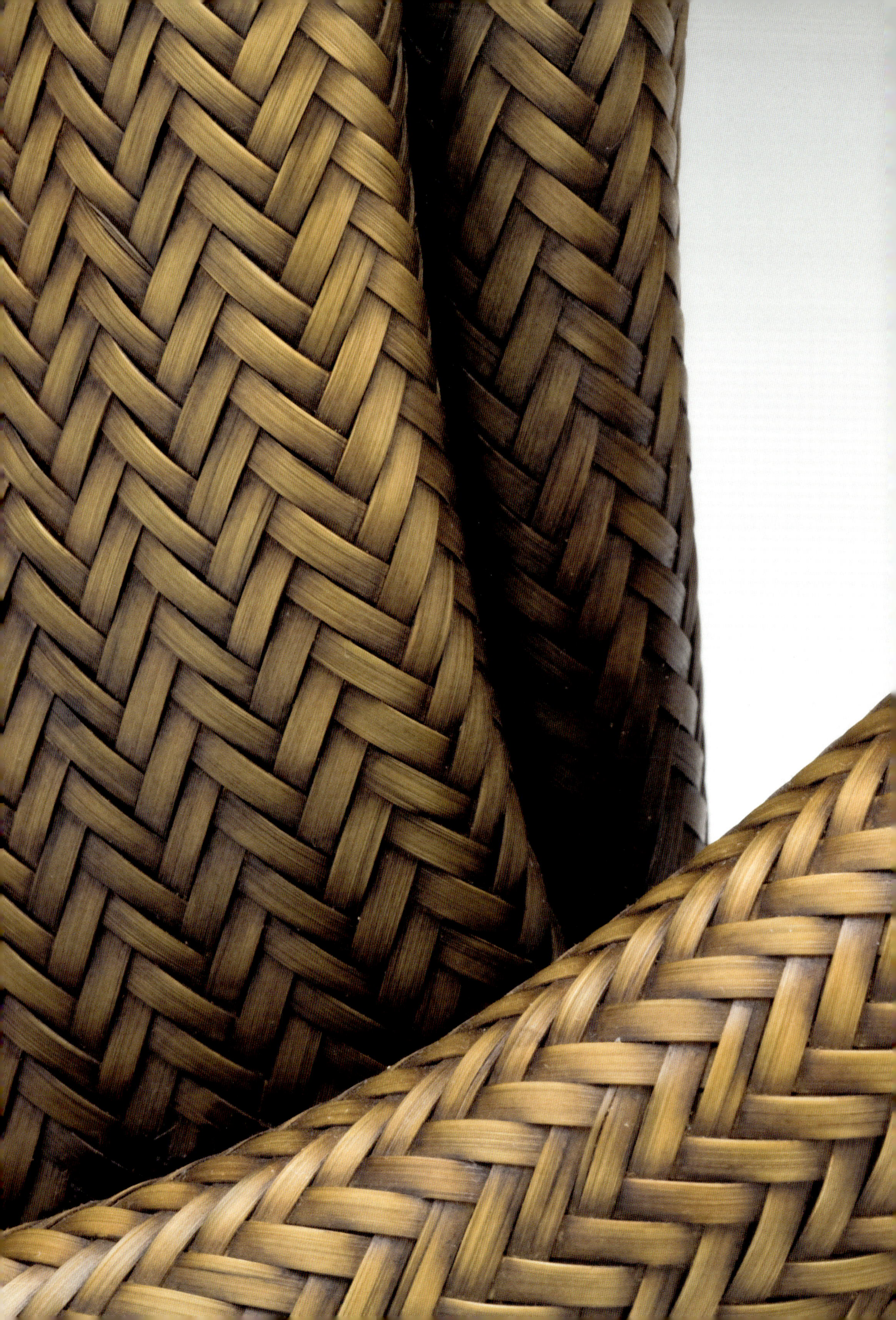

ENDNOTES

1 For information about Founders' Circle members' initial donations to the museum, see *An Inaugural Gift: Founders' Circle Collection* (Charlotte, NC: The Mint Museum of Craft + Design, 2000).

2 To celebrate the opening of the Mint Museum Uptown, and the new Craft + Design galleries, in October 2010, Project Ten Ten Ten was conceived as a way of dramatically updating and diversifying the holdings of the permanent collection of craft and design with a series of ten site-specific commissions. Makers were encouraged to take risks and embrace their big ideas. Each was required to supply a concept-to-completion video lasting between three and five minutes. Spearheaded by the MMCD Board of Directors, and funded by the museum's acquisitions endowment, the Board of Directors, affiliate groups, national organizations, and individual donors, Project Ten Ten Ten objects and installations display the tremendous creative energy of these makers. For more information about the project, see https://mintmuseum.org/project-ten-ten-ten/.

3 *Thicket* was a striking departure from Joyce's previous body of work. Its "offspring," a constellation of sculptures titled *Thicket II*, have been installed in front of the Center for Contemporary Art (CCA), in Santa Fe, New Mexico, since 2017.

4 Immanuel Kant, *Critique of Judgment*, trans. Werner Pluhar (Indianapolis: Hackett Publishing, 1987), 300.

5 Max Planck, *Scientific Autobiography and Other Papers* (New York: Philosophical Library, 1949), quoted in Robert Root-Bernstein and Michele Root-Bernstein, "The Art and Craft of Science," *Educational Leadership* 70, no. 5 (February 2013): 16–21, http://www.ascd.org/publications/educational-leadership/feb13/vol70/num05/The-Art-and-Craft-of-Science.aspx.

6 "What is Inquiry?" Institute for Inquiry, The Exploratorium, www.exploratorium.edu/ifi.

7 See Bronwyn Bevan, Mike Petrich, and Karen Wilkinson, "Tinkering is Serious Play," *Educational Leadership* 72, no. 4 (December 2014/January 2015): 28–33.

8 See Maikel Kuijpers, "Materials and Skills in the History of Knowledge: An Archaeological Perspective from the 'Non-Asian' Field," *Technology and Culture* 60, no. 2 (April 2019): 604–15.

9 All biographical details, unless otherwise noted, are from Oral history interview with Brent Kington, May 3–4, 2001, Archives of American Art, Smithsonian Institution, Washington, DC, https://www.si.edu/es/object/AAADCD_oh_226971. Kington earned a BFA (University of Kansas, 1957) and an MFA (Cranbrook Academy of Art, 1961) in metalsmithing.

10 Kington mostly learned from African American brothers Ben and Jim Deal, Murphysboro, Illinois. One of Kington's sources on ancient metalsmithing was *A History of Metallography* (University of Chicago Press, 1960), by Cyril Stanley Smith, whom Maikel Kuijpers also cites on the connection between craft, science, and technology in antiquity.

11 In 1969, Kington saw a television program about a man in Georgia who had written a book about blacksmithing by interviewing country blacksmiths. He invited the author, Alex Bealer, to join him in conducting the first workshop in 1970, later recounting that Bealer knew more than he did.

12 "L. Brent Kington (1934–2013)," *Metalsmith* 3, no. 5, 56.

13 Now called the American Folk Art Museum.

14 "By the time I got through the end of the series, I could predict within an eighth of an inch the balance point of the piece and where I had to punch the hole. . . . Then what attracted me to that was the fact that it could work with a large form and small form, creating illusions that would look like it shouldn't balance, but it did." Oral history interview with Brent Kington, May 3–4, 2001, Archives of American Art, Smithsonian Institution.

15 All biographical information from a studio visit with the artist on November 24, 2019 and from Andi Juell, "Interview with Elizabeth Brim," *Anvil Magazine*, April 1999, http://www.anvilmag.com/smith/brim.htm. Brim's jewelry instructor at Penland, Gary Noffke, took the class to the blacksmithing studio to make stakes to raise metal.

16 All information on Harling's process from Douglas Harling, "Uncommon Bonds," *The Penland Book of Jewelry* (Asheville, NC: Lark Books, 2004), 210–27.

17 All biographical information from Oral history interview with Paul Stankard, June 9–August 20, 2006, Archives of American Art, Smithsonian Institution, Washington, DC, https://www.aaa.si.edu/collections/interviews/oral-history-interview-paul-stankard-13579. Interestingly, it was Paul's father, a chemist, who recommended he study scientific glassblowing.

18 Glassmakers who were skilled at making lenses made the first microscope in 1590 and the first telescope in 1608, enabling the discovery of microbes, distant stars, and many other natural phenomena. Elsewhere in this volume, Dr. Hideo Mabuchi also comments on the importance of craft skills in his physics lab.

19 David Brand, "In New Jersey: Capturing Nature in Glass," *Time*, February 8, 1988, 12, 14. Failure could result from misalignment of the two gathers or from thermal shock that caused cracking during annealing, among other causes.

20 Andrew Buck, "Takeshi Yasuda," *Ceramics Technical* 36 (2013): 72–76.

21 Yasuda makes a similar bowl in "Takeshi Yasuda: Made in China," https://www.youtube.com/watch?v=9MSxEAekY1U&t=138s.

22 https://nanocomposix.com/pages/gold-nanoparticles-optical-properties#target.

23 Oral history with David Ellsworth, Archives of American Art, Smithsonian Institution, Washington, DC, July 16, 2007, https://www.aaa.si.edu/collections/interviews/oral-history-interview-david-ellsworth-13679; see also "Woodturner David Ellsworth at the Philadelphia Museum of Art," https://www.youtube.com/watch?v=IP10cVILW5c&t=67s.

24 All information about making *Pike Basking* from a studio visit with the artist, January 27, 2020.

25 Artist's website, http://www.donaldfortescue.com/about; http://www.donaldfortescue.com/new-page-2 (résumé).

26 Christie van der Haak, "Fairy Tales/Sproken," in Jane Huldman and Philip Peters, eds., *Christie van der Haak: Sproken/Fairy Tales*, trans. Marie Louise Schoondergang, Ulrica Yland, and Willem Kramer (The Hague: Stroom den Haag; Heijningen: Jap Sam Books, 2015), 15–16.

27 Diana Daniel, "A Dutch Laboratory that Paints in Yarn," *New York Times*, December 5, 2018.

28 Rolf Fehlbaum, "Nature: Image or Model?," http://www.bouroullec.com/upload/facsimile/vegetal.pdf.

29 Ronan and Erwan Bouroullec, "Growing a Chair," http://www.bouroullec.com/upload/facsimile/vegetal.pdf.

30 The *Vegetal Chair* won the ICFF (International Contemporary Furniture Fair) award for outdoor furniture in 2009.

31 Artist's website, http://www.tom-price.com/about-1.

32 All technical information from www.yellowtrace.com.au/tom-price-synthesis/.

33 Artist's website, http://www.tom-price.com/synthesis-info.

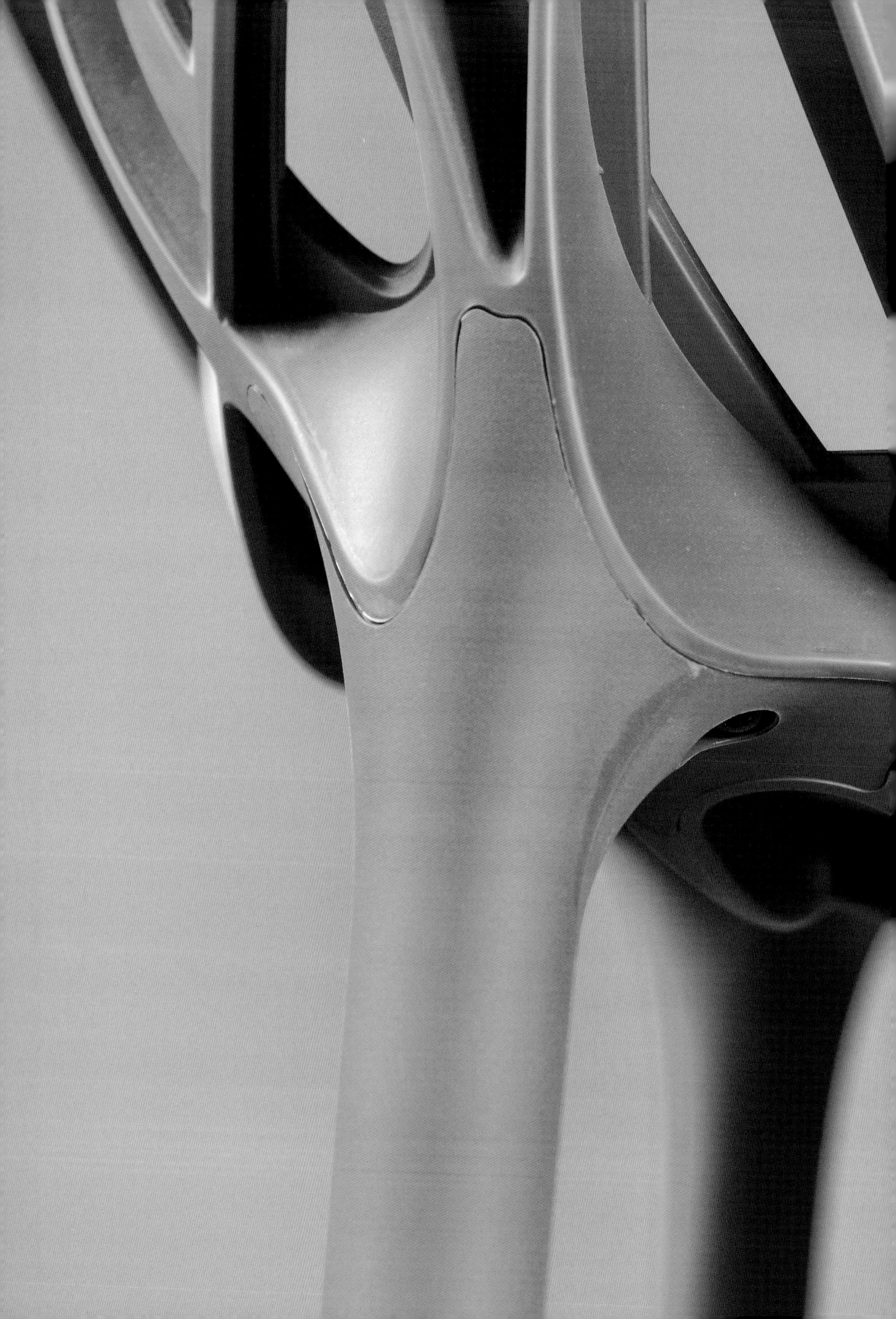

CATALOGUE

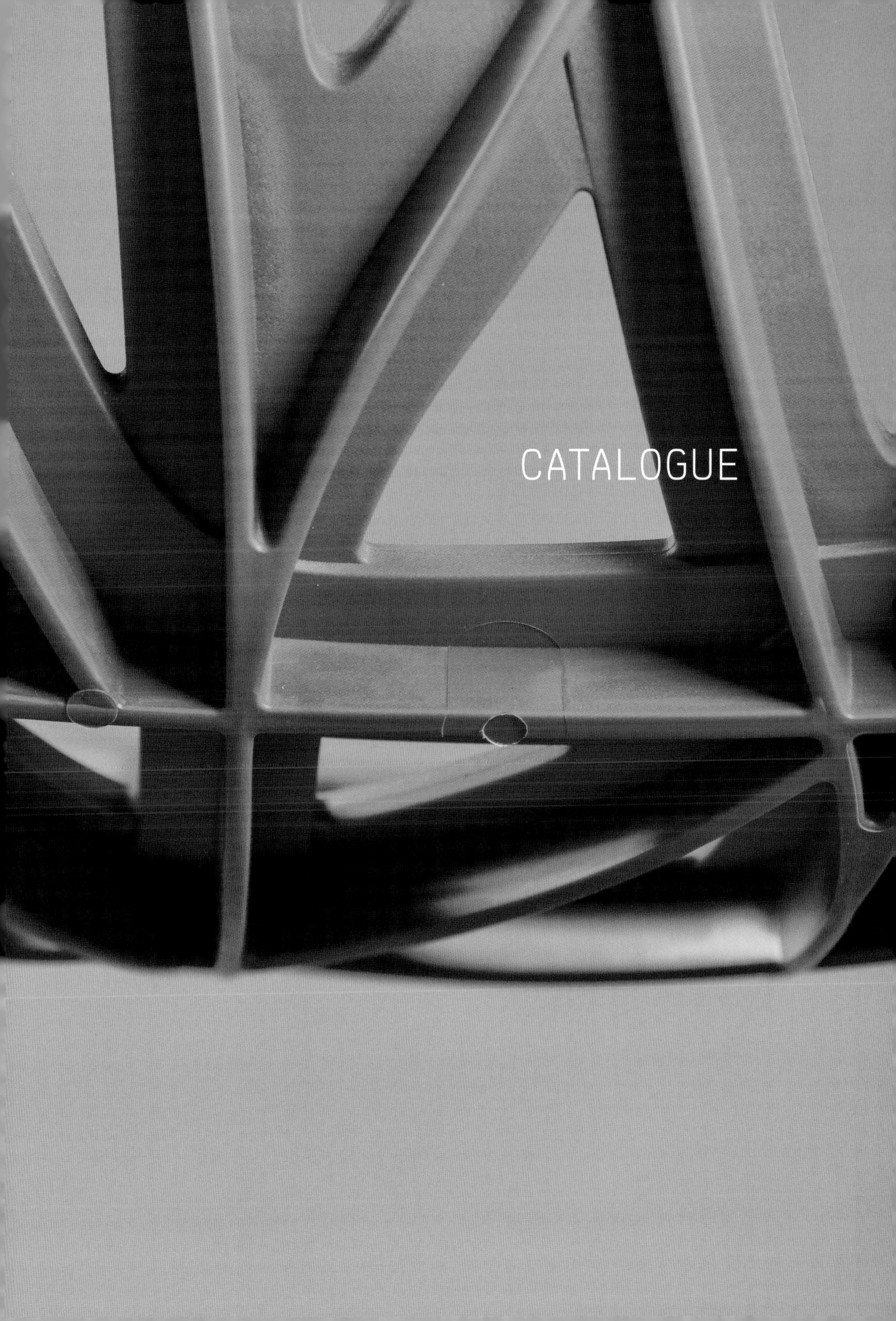

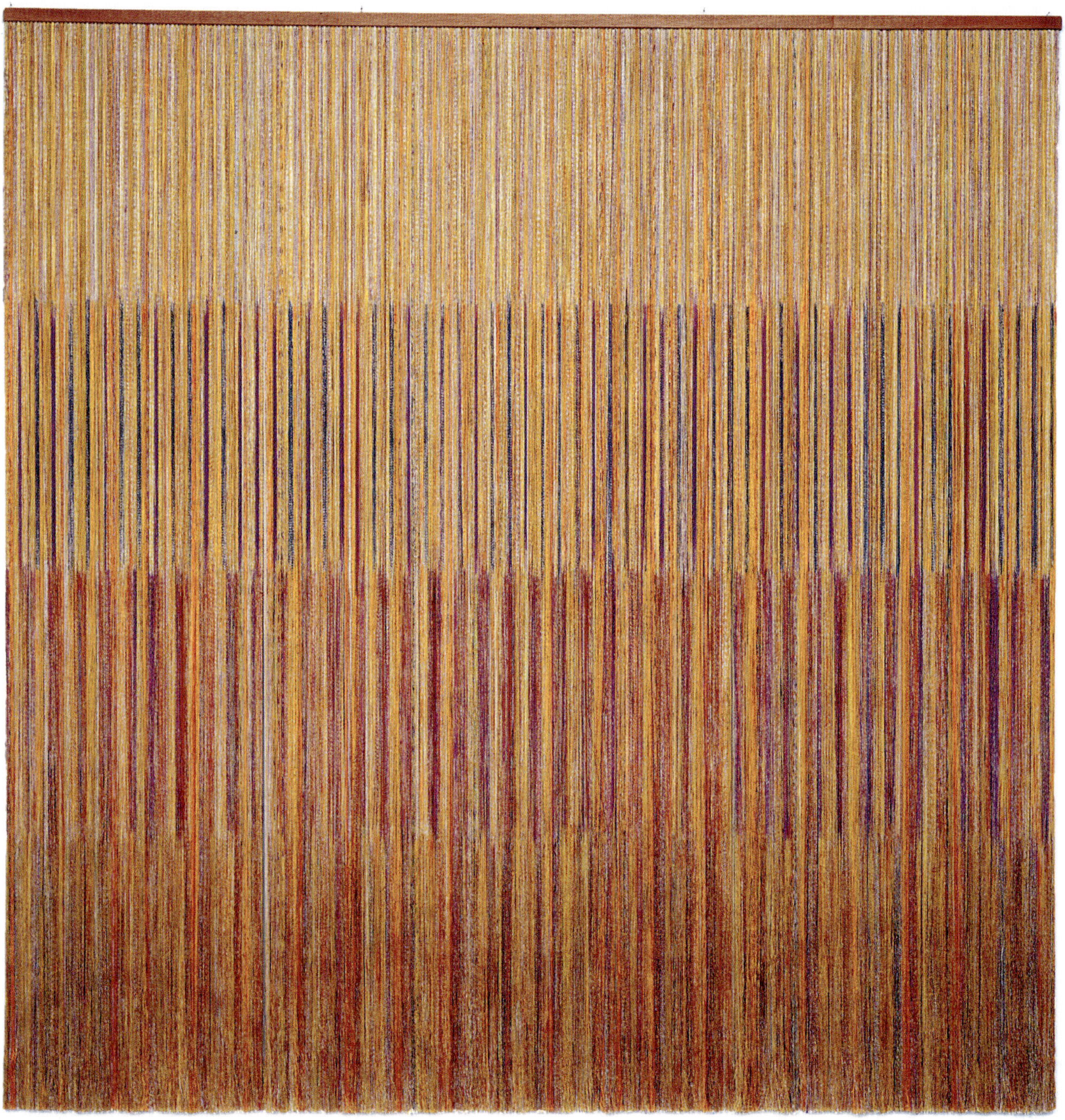

CAT. 1

Ulla-Maija Vikman (Finnish, 1943–).
***11313322*, 1999, viscose thread,**
mahogany, 79" x 79".

Gift of Virginia Kemp in memory
of Francis B. Kemp. 2008.46.
© 1999, 11313322

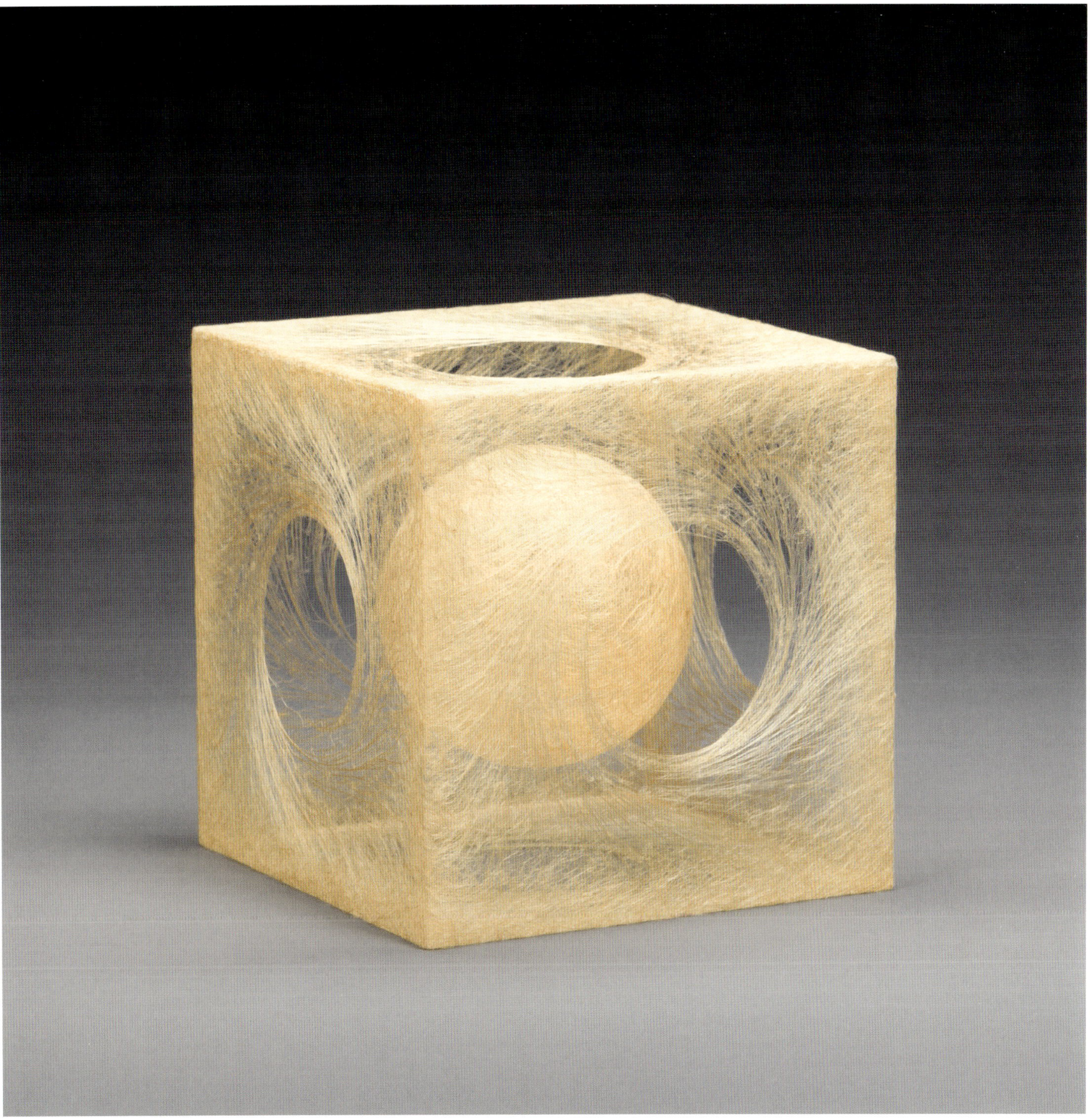

CAT. 2
Naoko Serino (Japanese, 1962–).
***Jute Square*, 2006, jute, 10" x 10" x 10".**
Gift of Lorne Lassiter and Gary Ferraro. 2017.5.18
Photo: Keara Reburn

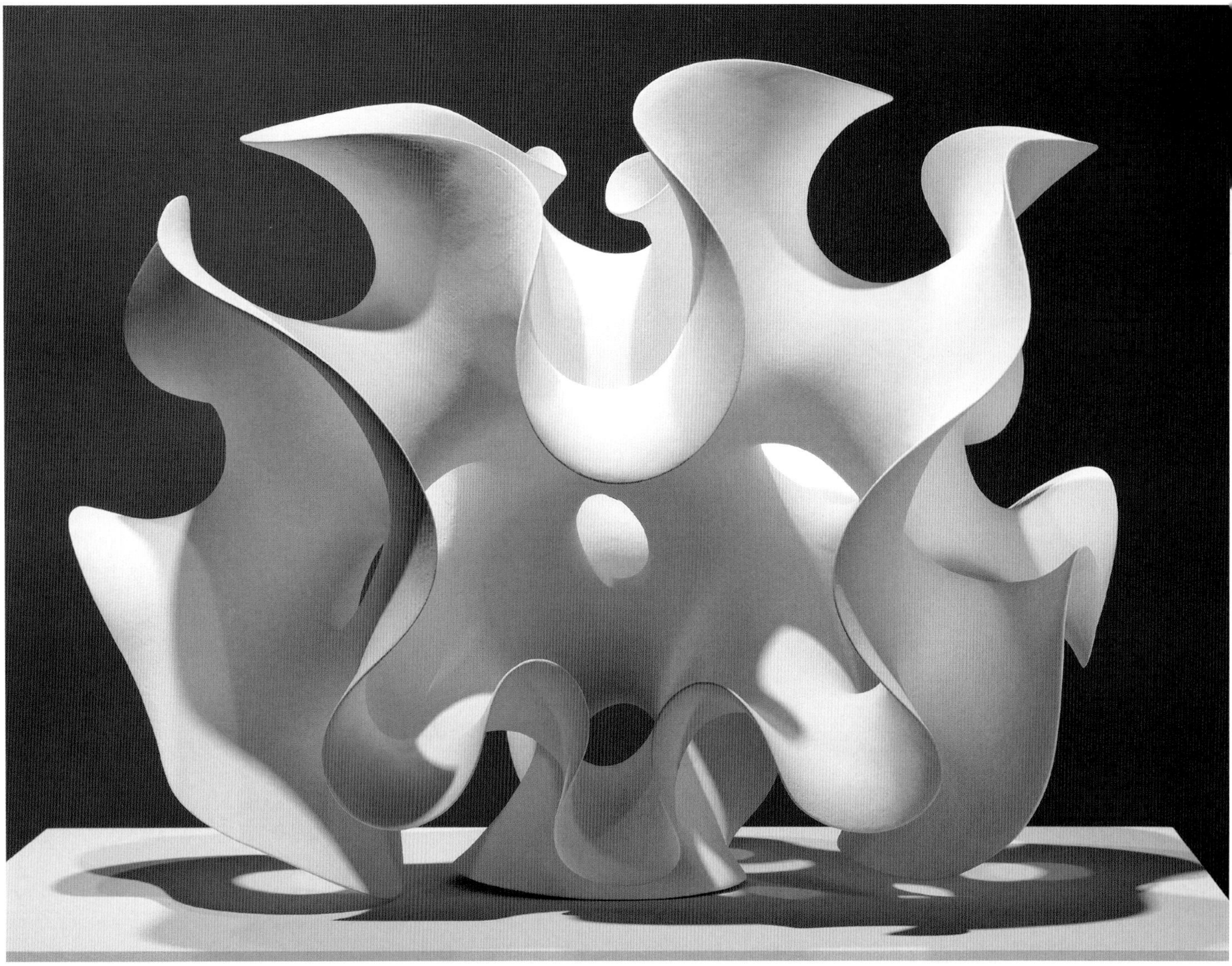

CAT. 3

Eva Hild (Swedish, 1966–).
***Flutter*, 2004–5, hand-coiled and sanded stoneware, kaolin slip, mixed media, 23" x 30" x 26".**
Museum Purchase: Windgate Fund. 2005.61.
© Flutter, 2005, Stoneware, Eva Hild
Photo: Mitchell Kearney

CAT. 4

Eleanor Lakelin (British, 1960–).
***Echoes of Amphora: III/18*, 2018, lathe-turned, hollowed, sand-blasted, and bleached horse chestnut burl wood, 20.87" x 16.93" x 16.93".**
Museum Purchase with funds from the Charles W. Beam Accessions Endowment. 2019.1
Photo: Brandon Scott

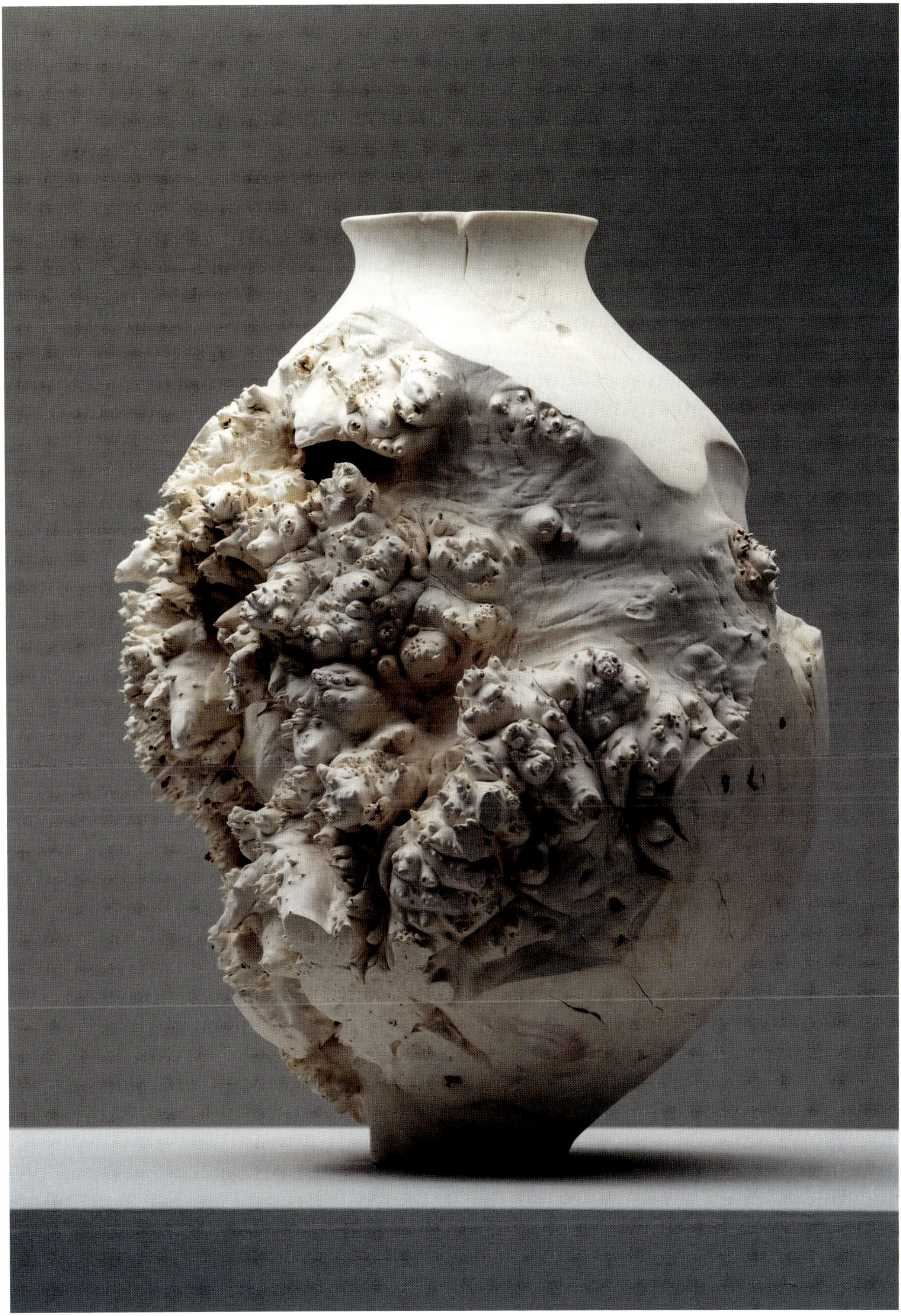

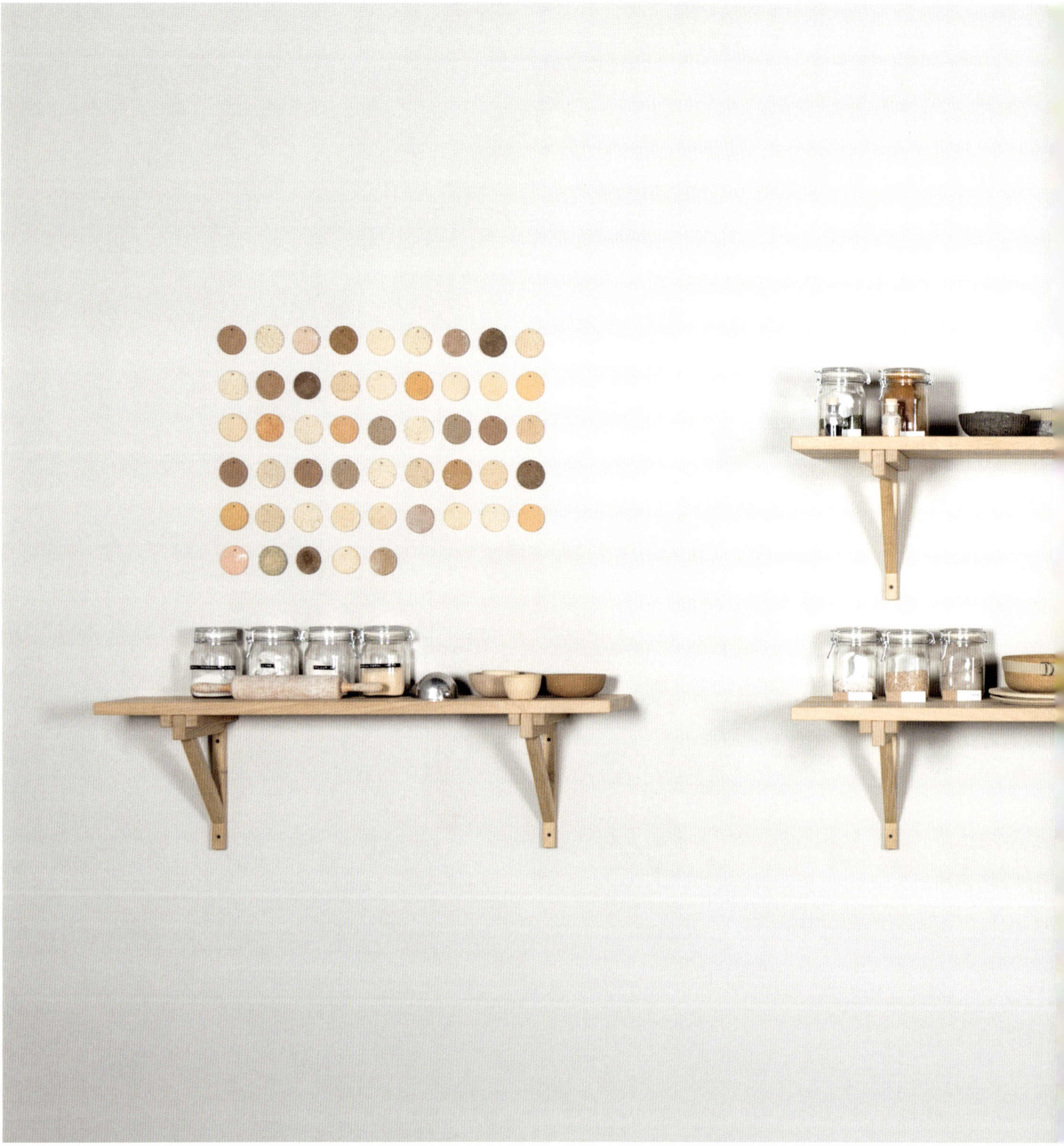

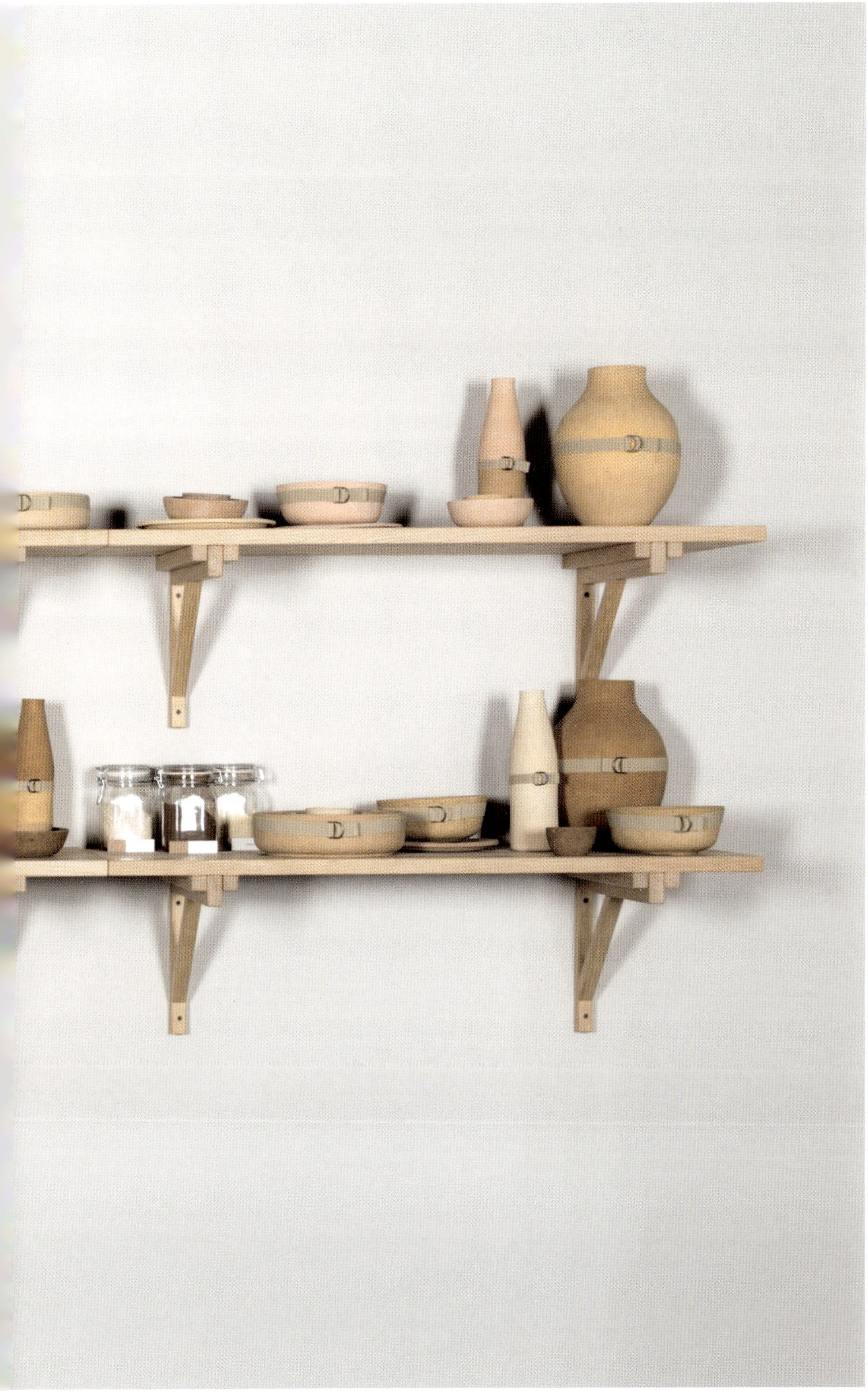

CAT. 5

Studio Formafantasma (Eindhoven, The Netherlands, 2009–), Andrea Trimarchi (Italian, 1983–), Simone Farresin (Italian, 1980–). *Autarchy*, 2012, flour, agricultural waste, vegetable dye, beeswax, pine tar, 49" x 156.25" x 18.75".

Museum Purchase: Funds provided by Missy Luczak Smith and Doug Smith. 2013.18.1-158
Photo: Keara Reburn

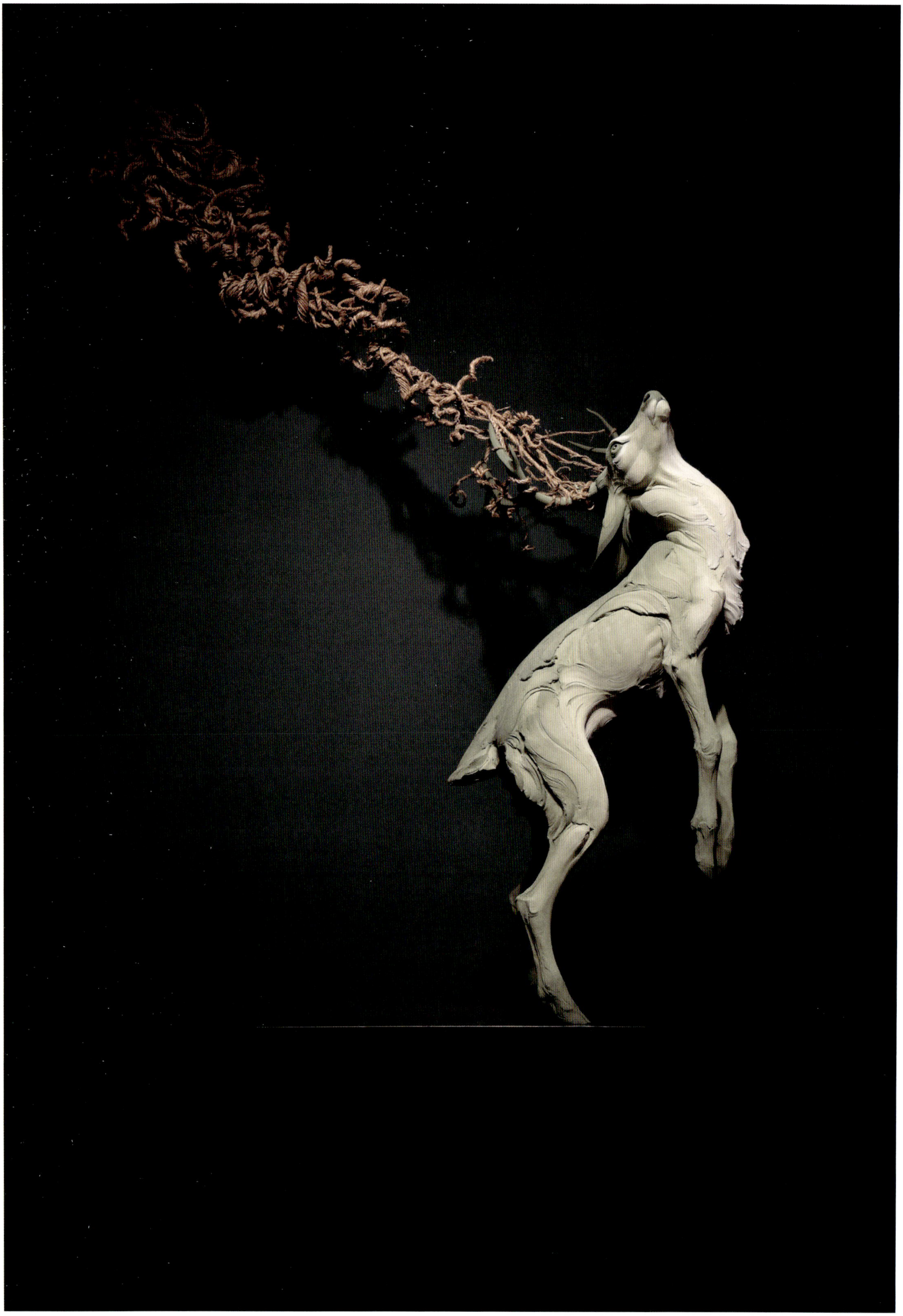

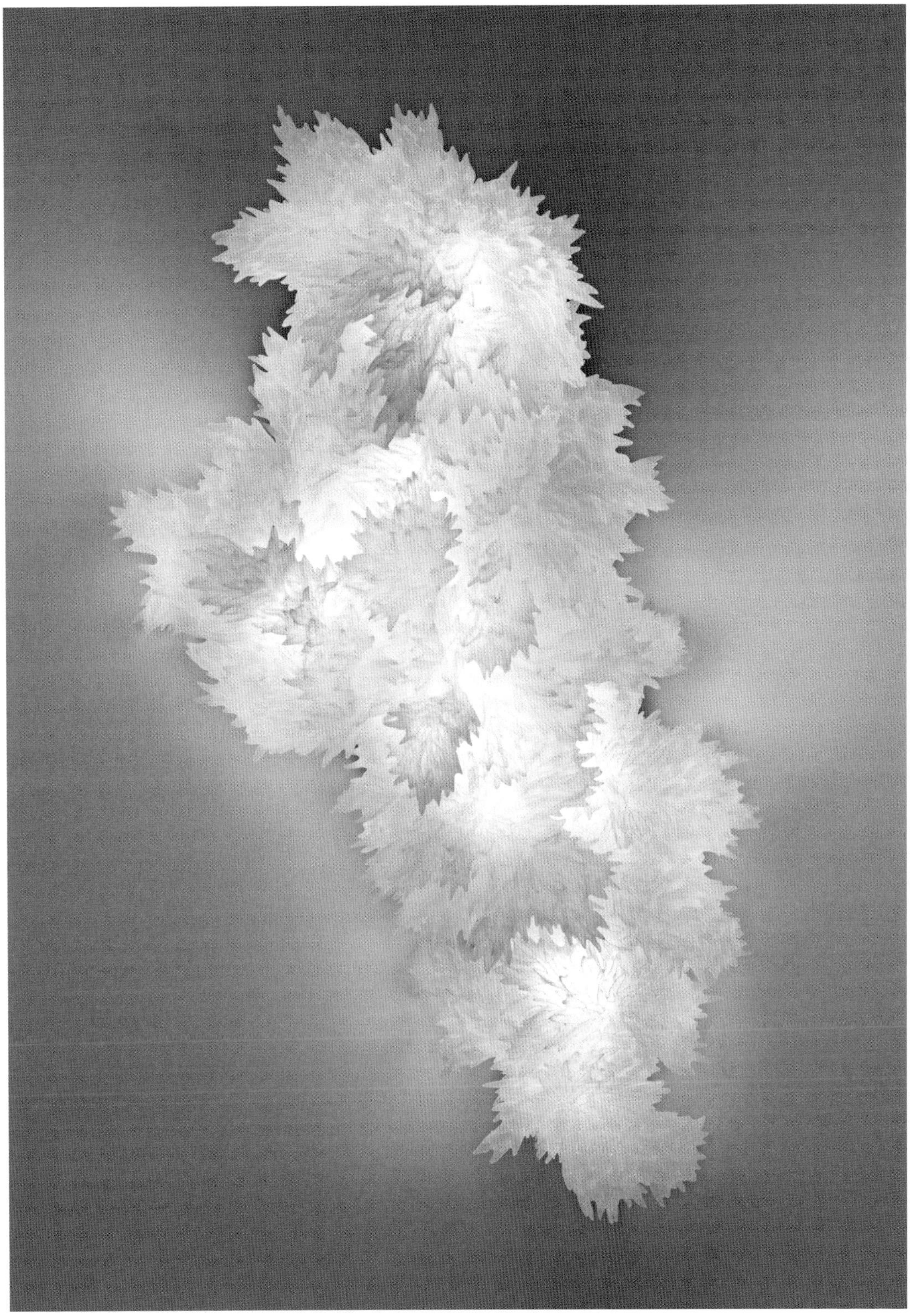

CAT. 6

Beth Cavener (American, 1972–).
***Beloved (Rearing Deer)*, 2017,**
stoneware, bone, fiber, steel,
105" x 54" x 30".

Museum Purchase: Funds provided by Charles W. Beam Accessions Endowment, Judy and John Alexander, Bill Gorelick, Mint Museum Auxiliary, Laura and Mike Grace, Lorne Lassiter and Gary Ferraro, Jacqueline and Sean Jones, Betsy and Dr. Brian Wilder, and Hillary and Fairfax Cooper. 2019.97A-C
Photo: Brandon Scott

CAT. 7

Ayala Serfaty (Israeli, 1962–).
***Joy of Transition*, 2012, lampworked glass, polymer, 72" x 40" x 20".**

Project Ten Ten Ten commission. Museum Purchase: Founders' Circle 2011 Annual Cause. DVD produced with additional funds from the Association of Israel's Decorative Arts (AIDA). 2012.80A-B. © Ayala Serfaty 2012

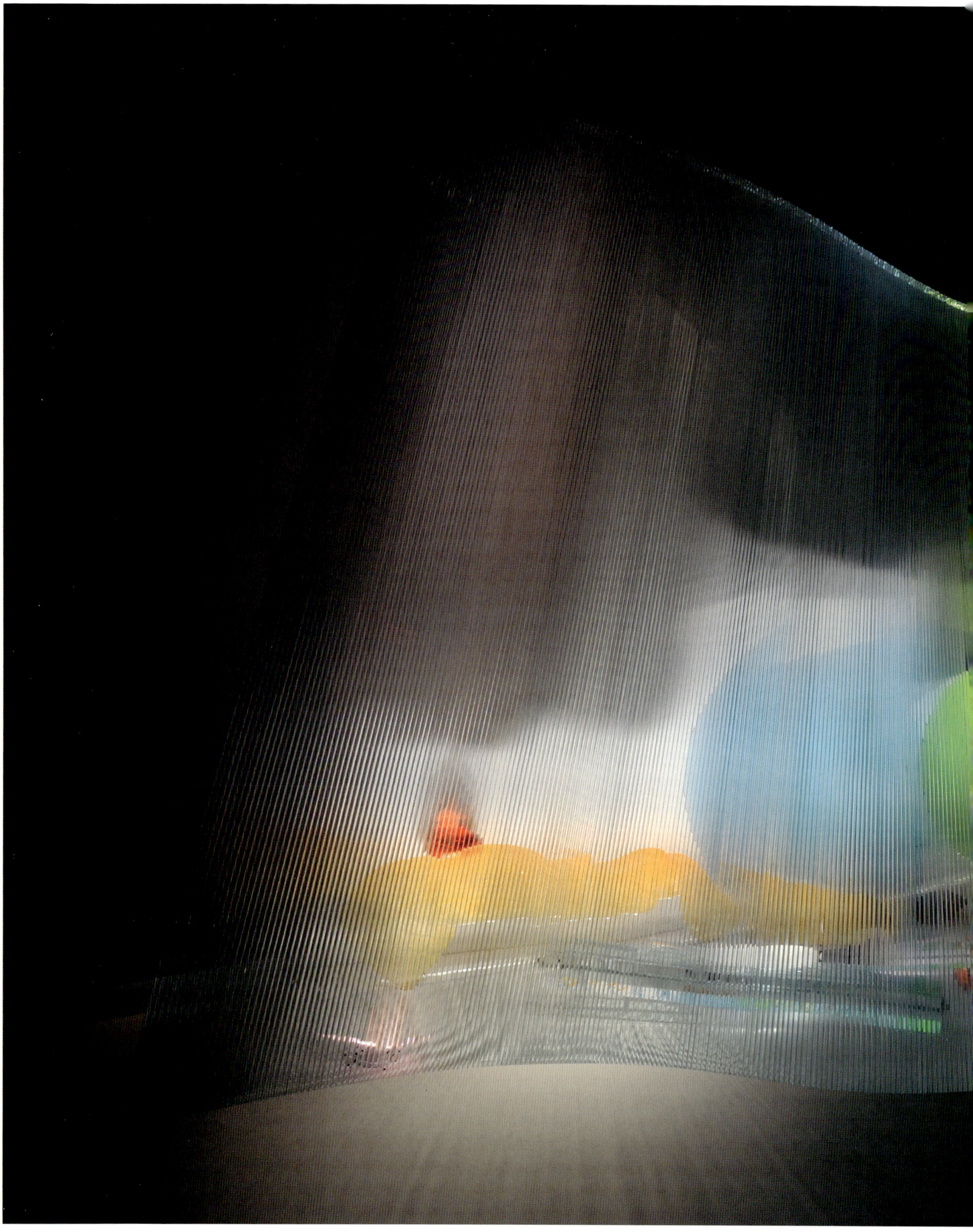

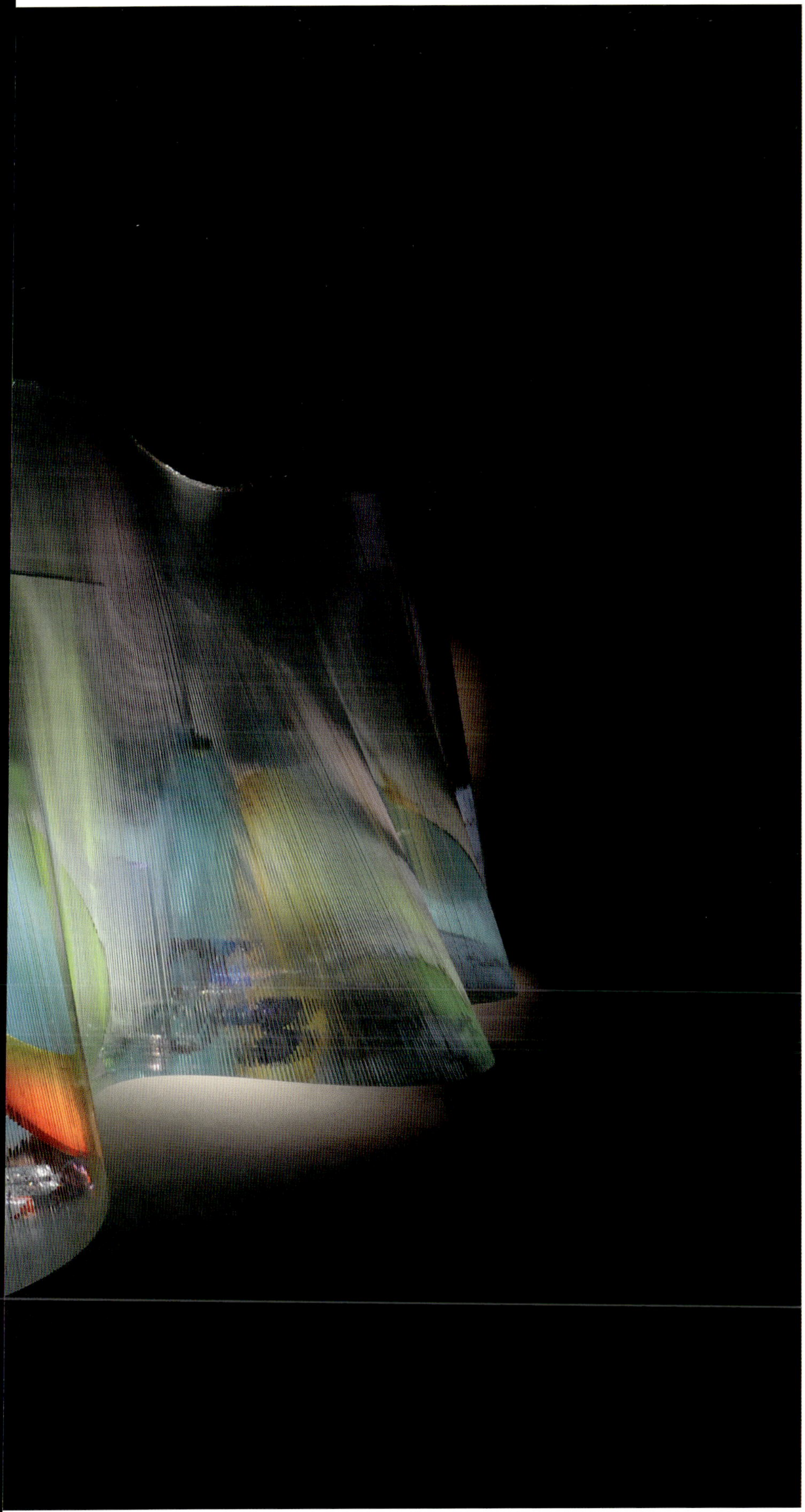

CAT. 8

Danny Lane (American, 1955–).
***Threshold*, 2010, stacked plate glass, molded glass, steel, 112" x 321" x 58".**

Project Ten Ten Ten Commission. Museum Purchase: Exchange funds from various donors; Gift of William and Patty Gorelick, Drew and Beth Quartapella, Shelton and Carol Gorelick, John and Stacy Sumner Jesso, Richard and Yvonne McCracken, and the Founders' Circle Cause 2009 contributors. 2010.70.
© Danny Lane, 2010
Photo: Peter Wood

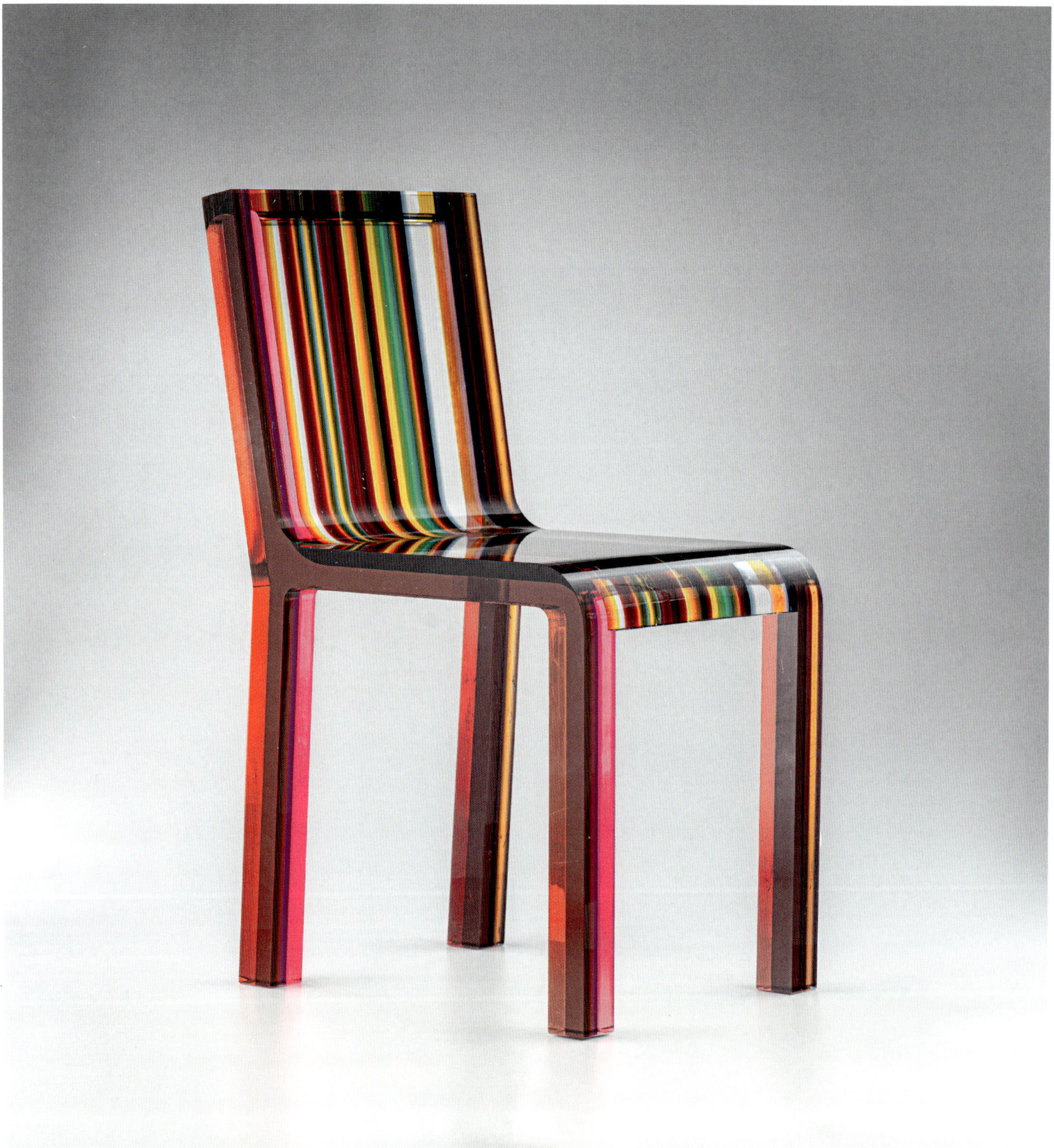

CAT . 9
**Patrick Norguet (French, 1969–),
Cappellini (Italy, 1946–).
Rainbow Chair, 2000, acrylic,
31.5" x 15.125" x 19.5".**
Gift of Larry Brady. 2019.92.3
Photo: Brandon Scott

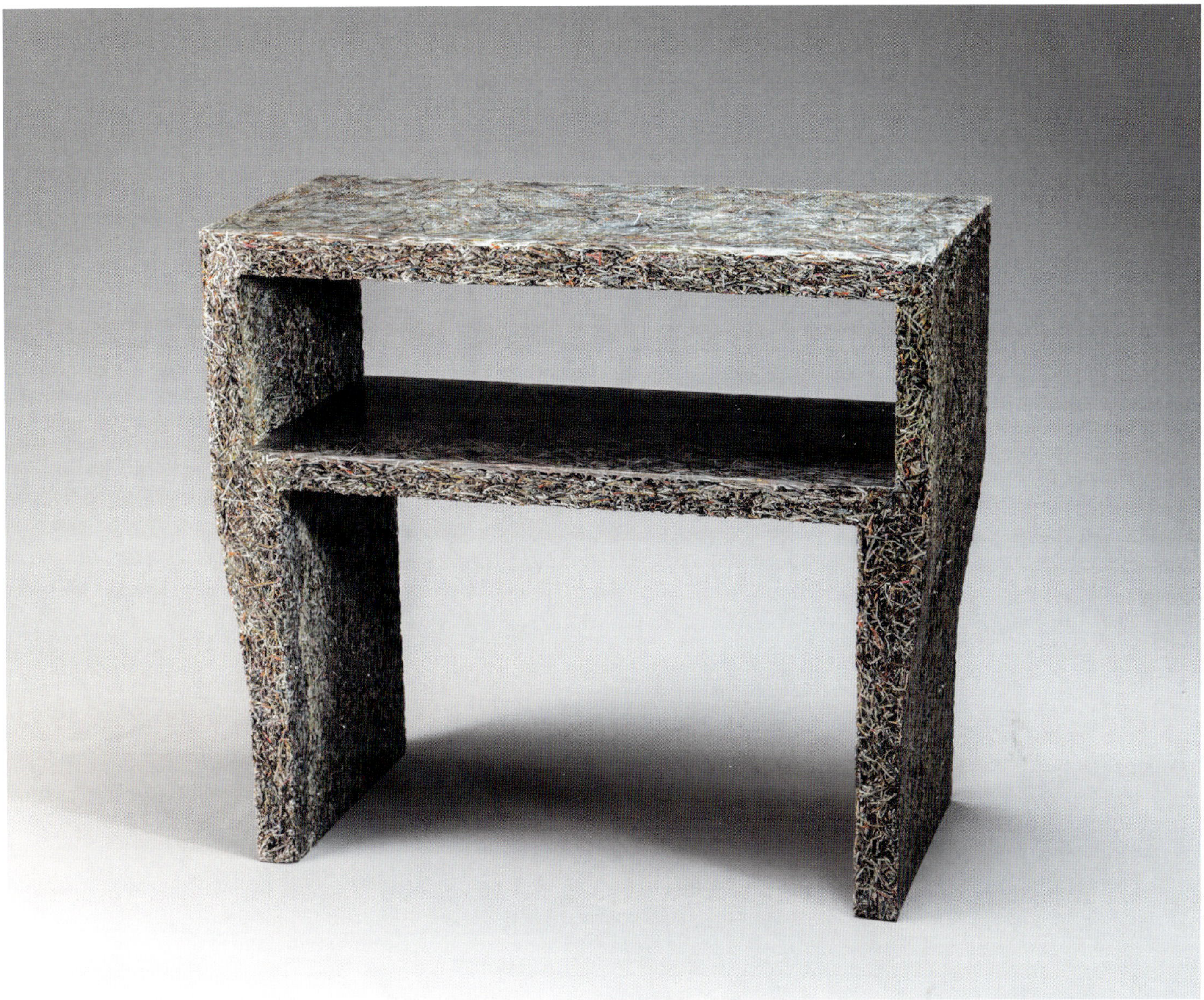

CAT. 10

Jens Praet (Belgian, 1984–). *Shredded Side Table (Harper's Bazaar Interiors Edition)*, 2013, shredded paper in resin, aluminum, 29.625" x 30.875" x 15.75".

Gift of Design Days Dubai and the Artist through Industry Gallery. 2015.1. © Jens Praet 2013
Photo: Brandon Scott

CAT. 11

Joseph Walsh (Irish, 1979–).
***Enignum Motion*, 2010, assembled, bleached, and oiled ash wood, lacquer, 48" x 120" x 19".**

Project Ten Ten Ten commission. Museum Purchase: Funds provided by the Board of Directors of the Mint Museum of Craft + Design: Laura Babb Grace and Mike Grace, Patty and Bill Gorelick, Paige and Hall Johnston, Deidre and Clay Grubb, Jeff Fagan, Jackie and Mike Wells, Patti Tracey and Chris Hudson, Shelly and Adam Landau, Libba and Mike Gaither, Susan and Loy McKeithen, Barbara and Jim Jamison, Arlene and Eric Oppenheim, and the Founders' Circle Cause 2009 contributors. 2010.85.

Photo: Mitchell Kearney

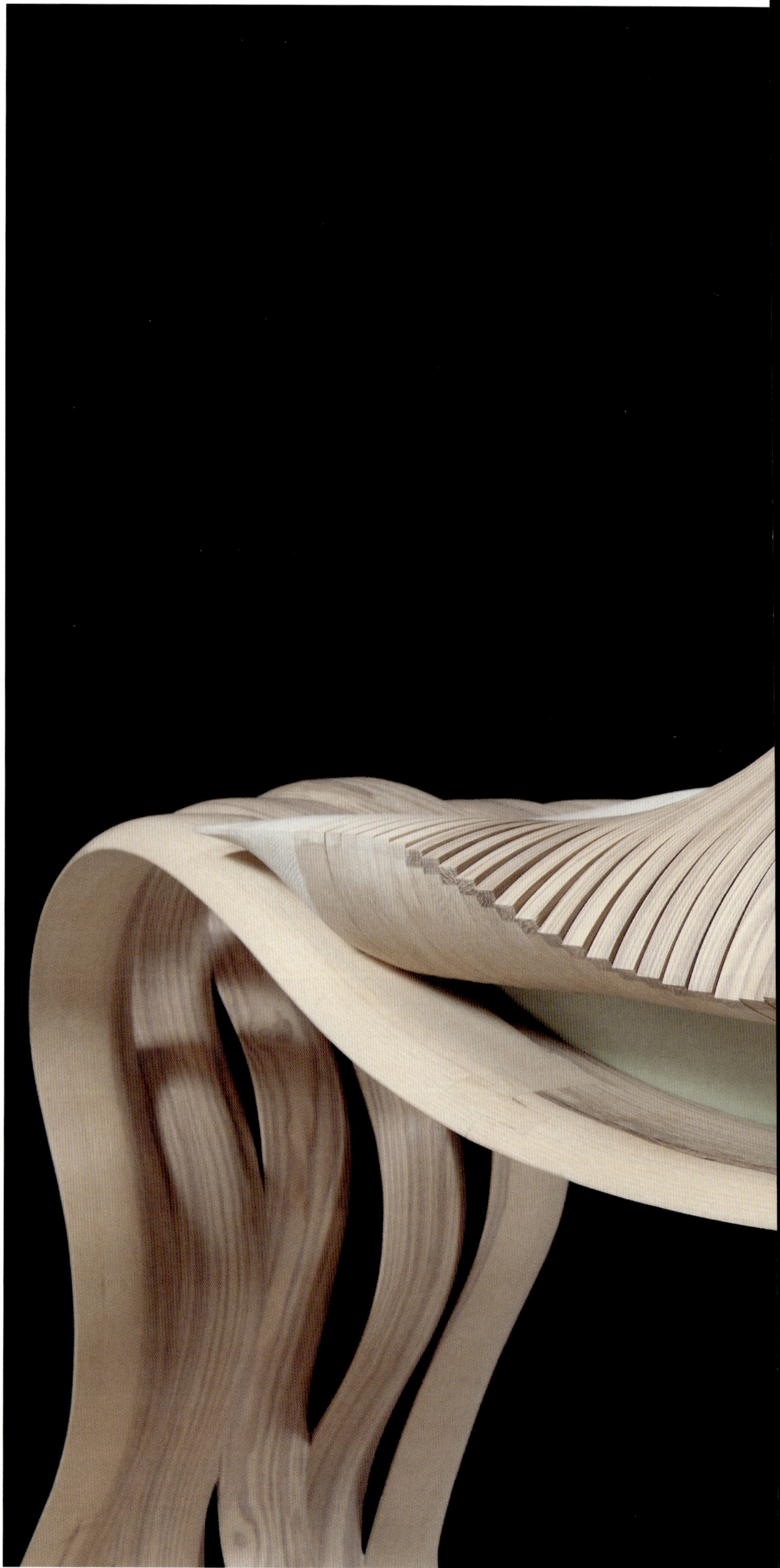

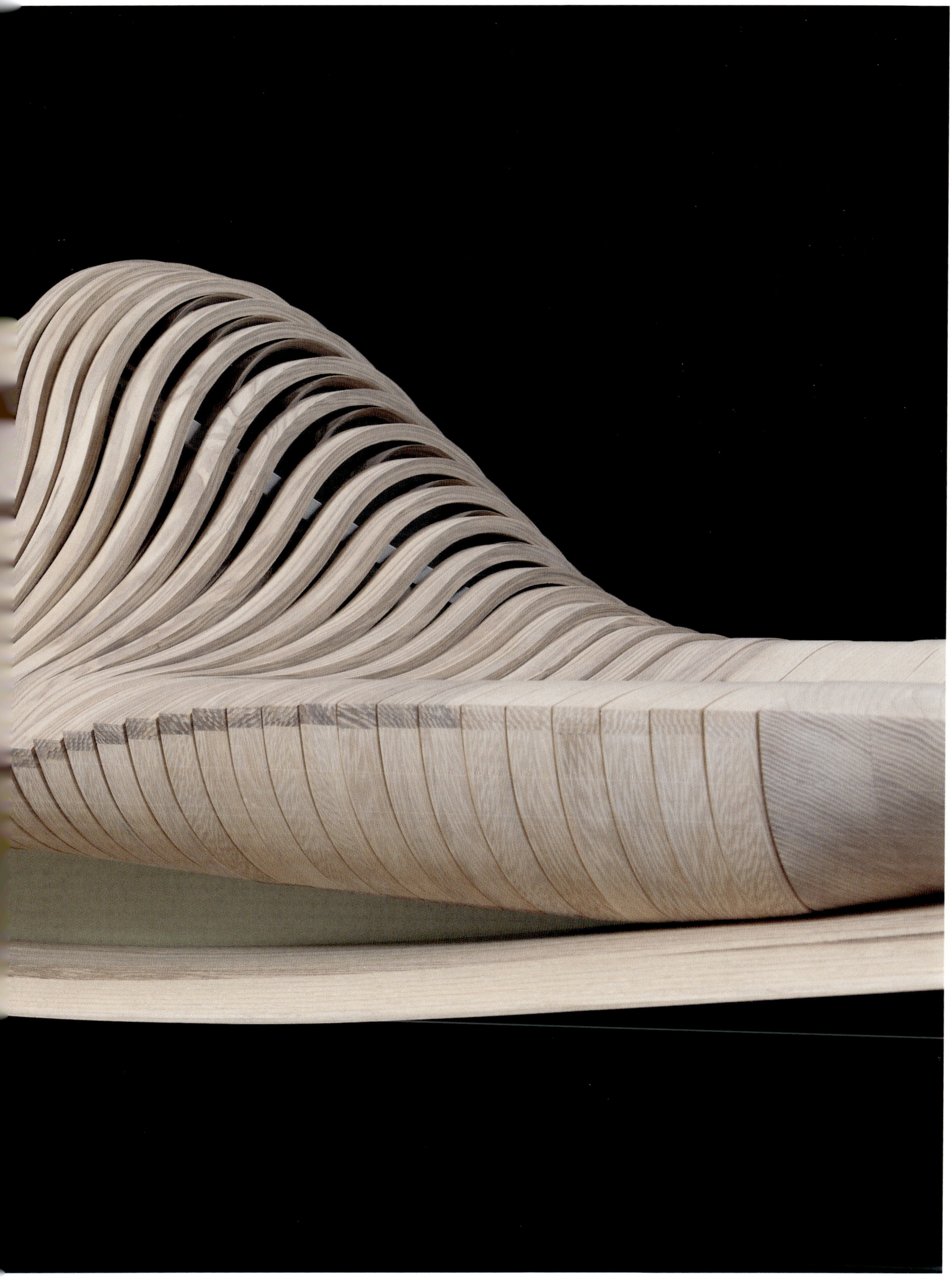

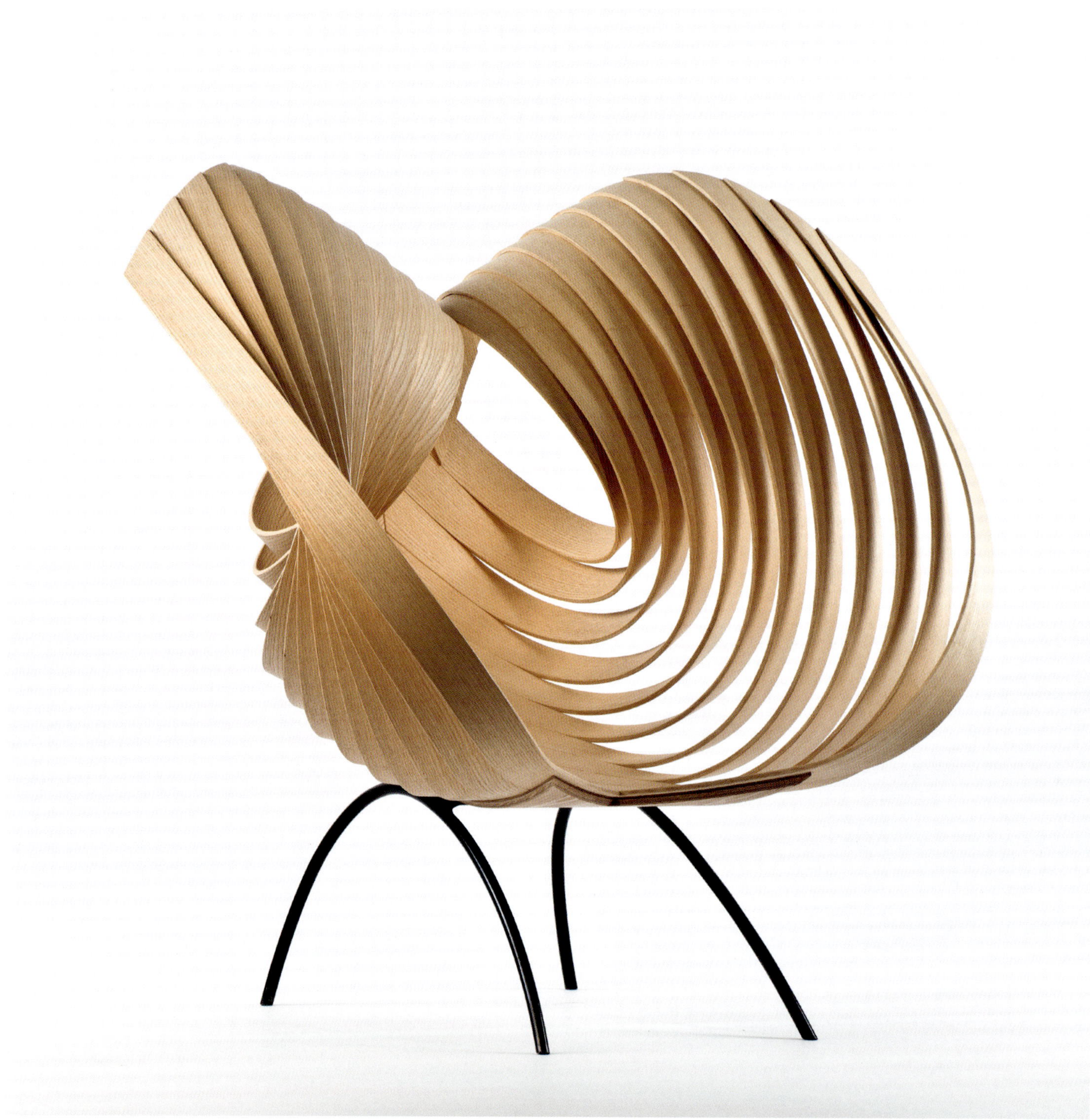

CAT. 12

Laura Kishimoto (American, 1991–).
***Yumi Chair II*, 2014, wood veneer, steel, 47" x 48" x 41".**

Promised gift, The Thomas H. and Diane DeMell Jacobson Ph.D. Foundation. L2019.9.4
Image courtesy Laura Kishimoto and KeneK Photography

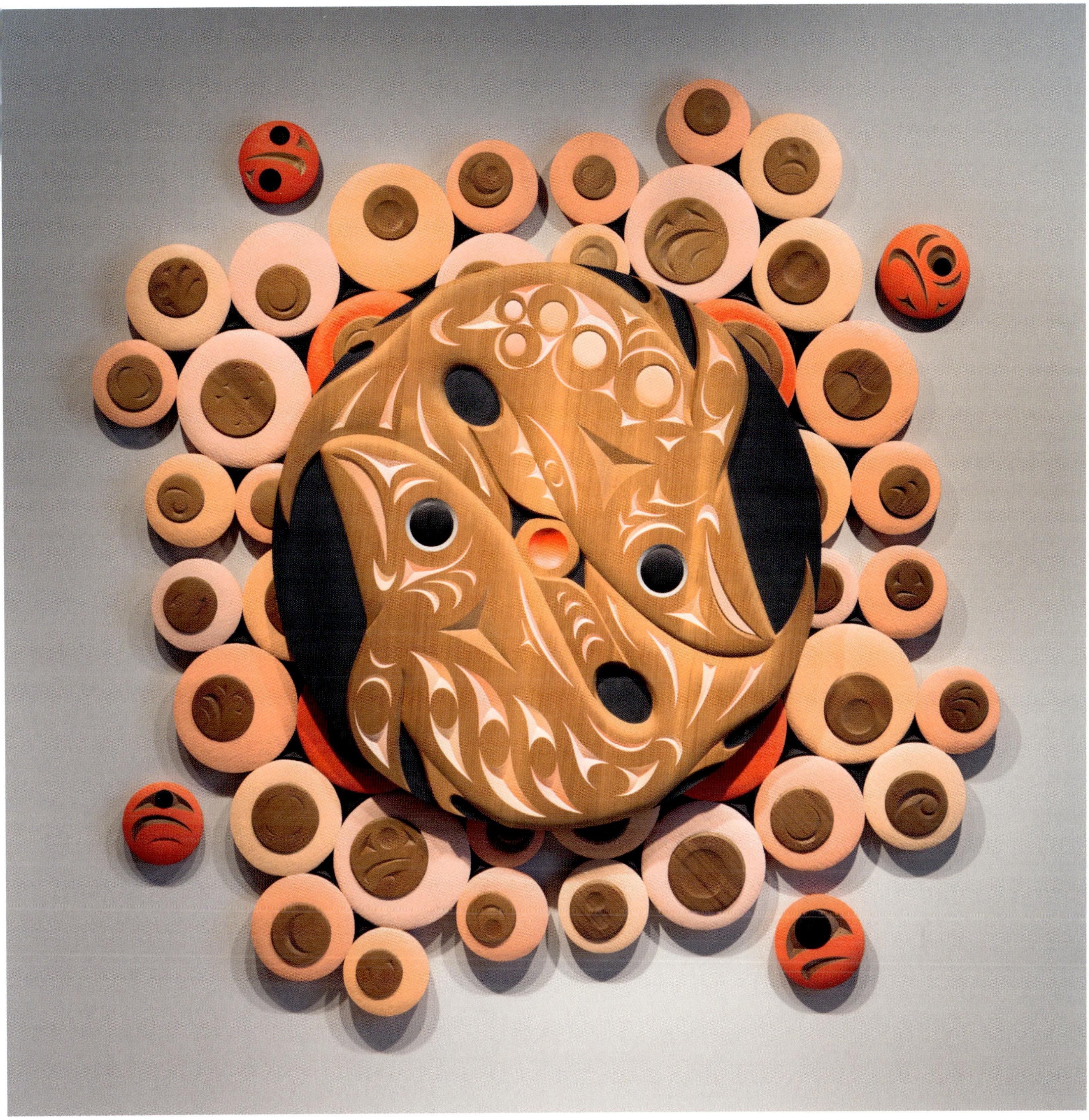

CAT. 13

Susan Point (Canadian, Coast Salish [Musqueam First Nation], 1952–). *Salmon Spawning Run*, 2012, carved and painted Western red cedar, 84" x 78".

Project Ten Ten Ten commission. Museum Purchase: Funds provided by Fleur Bresler, Libba and Mike Gaither, Laura and Mike Grace, Betsy and Brian Wilder, Amy and Alfred Dawson, Aida and Greg Saul, Missy Luczak Smith and Doug Smith, Beth and Drew Quartapella, and Kim Blanding. 2012.107A-I. © Susan Point 2012 Photo: Brandon Scott

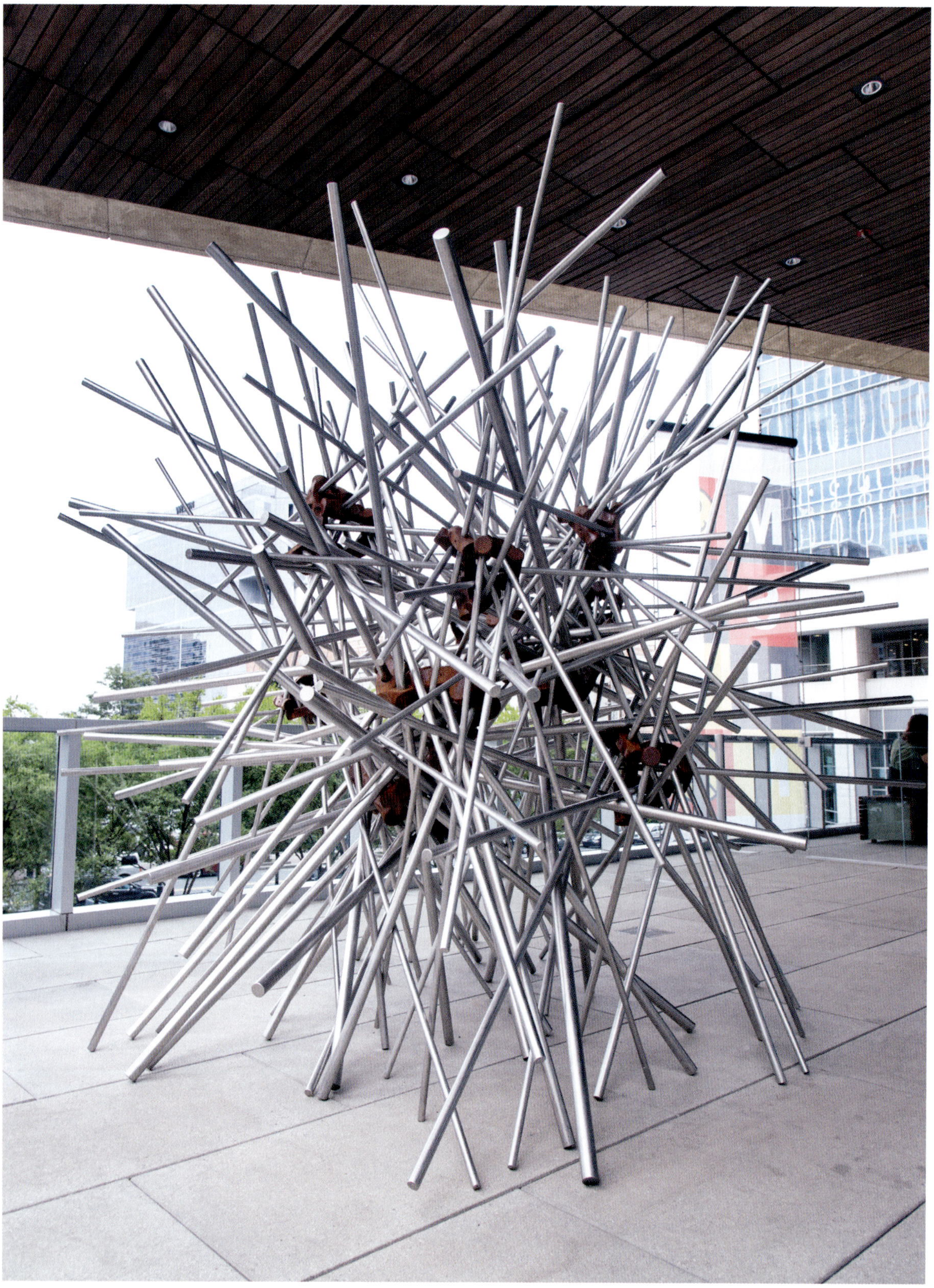

CAT. 14

Tom Joyce (American, 1956–), *Thicket*, 2015, stainless steel, cast iron, 94" x 92" x 90".

Project Ten Ten Ten commission. Museum Purchase: Funds provided by the Mint Museum Auxiliary in honor of Sally Van Allen. 2015.22. © Tom Joyce, 2015 Photo: Keara Reburn

CAT. 15

Ted Noten (Dutch, 1956–). *Slow: Eleven Women and 400 Daisies,* 2010, 3D-printed and gold-plated nylon, magnetized plastic daisies, 17" x 12.5" x 16.375".

Project Ten Ten Ten Commission. Museum Purchase: Funds provided by the Mint Museum Auxiliary. 2010.84. © 2010 Atelier Ted Noten Photo: Mitchell Kearney

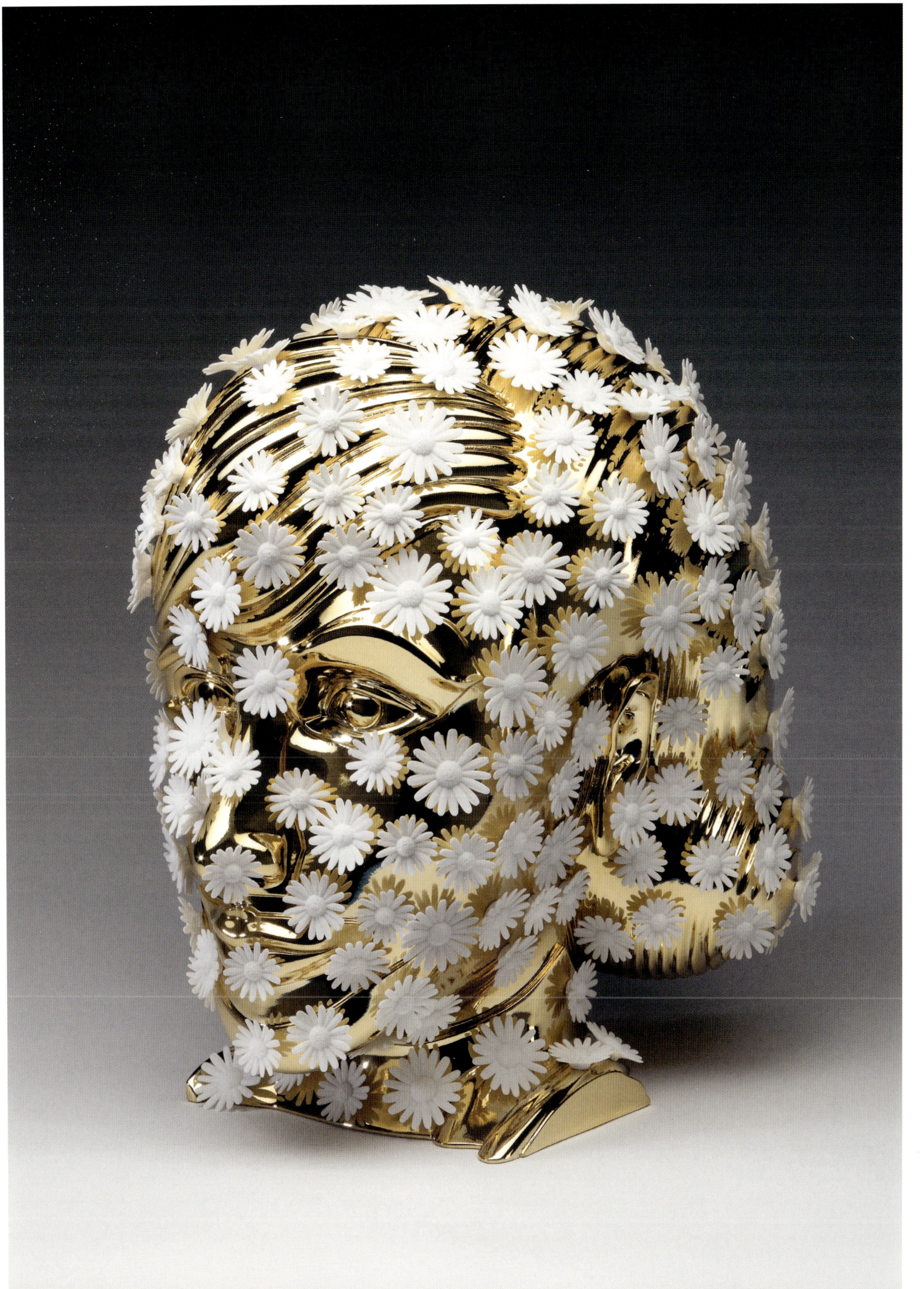

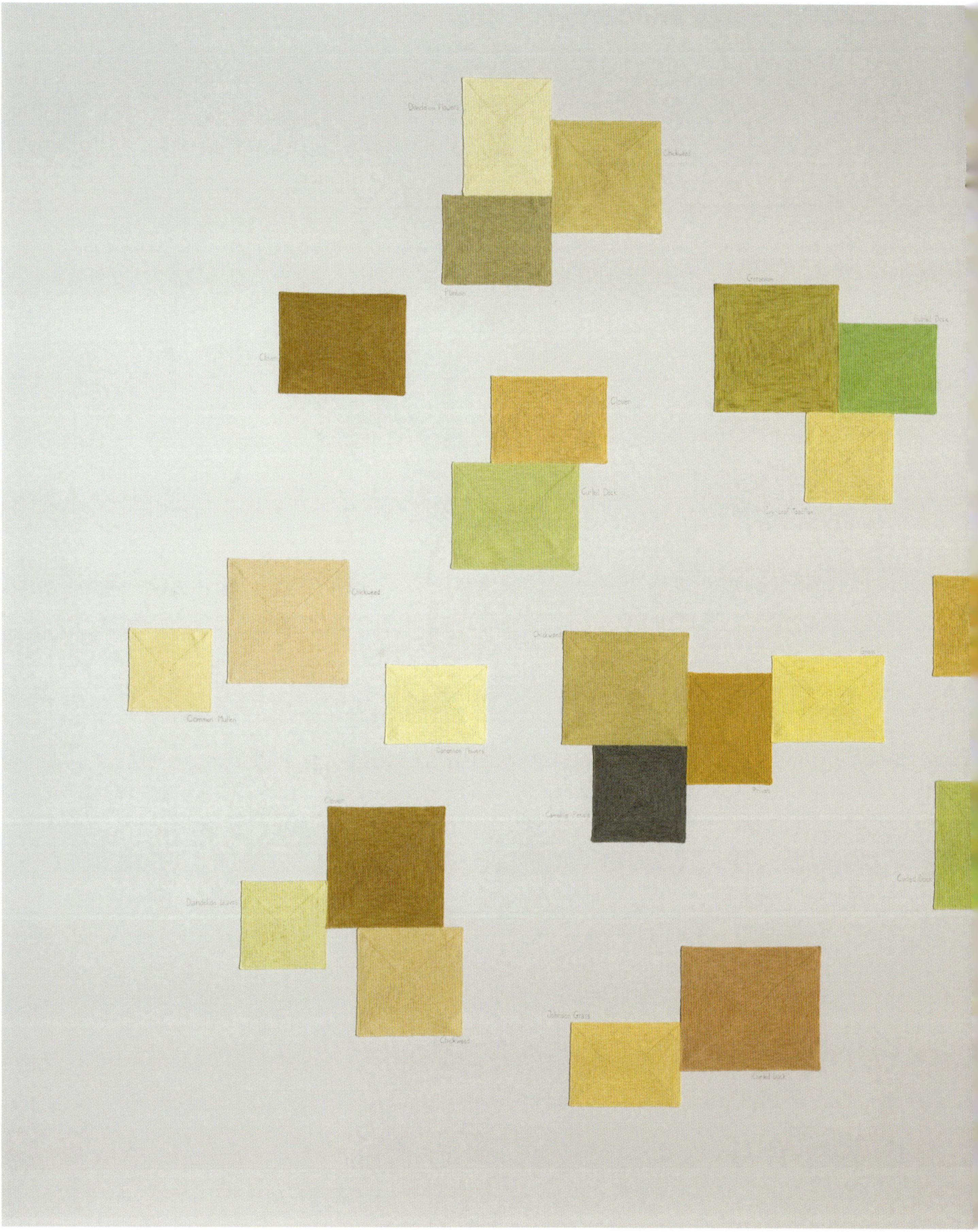
Dandelion Flowers
Chickweed
Plantain
Clover
Clover
Curled Dock
Chickweed
Common Mullen
Chickweed
Clover
Dandelion Leaves
Chickweed
Johnson Grass
Curled Dock

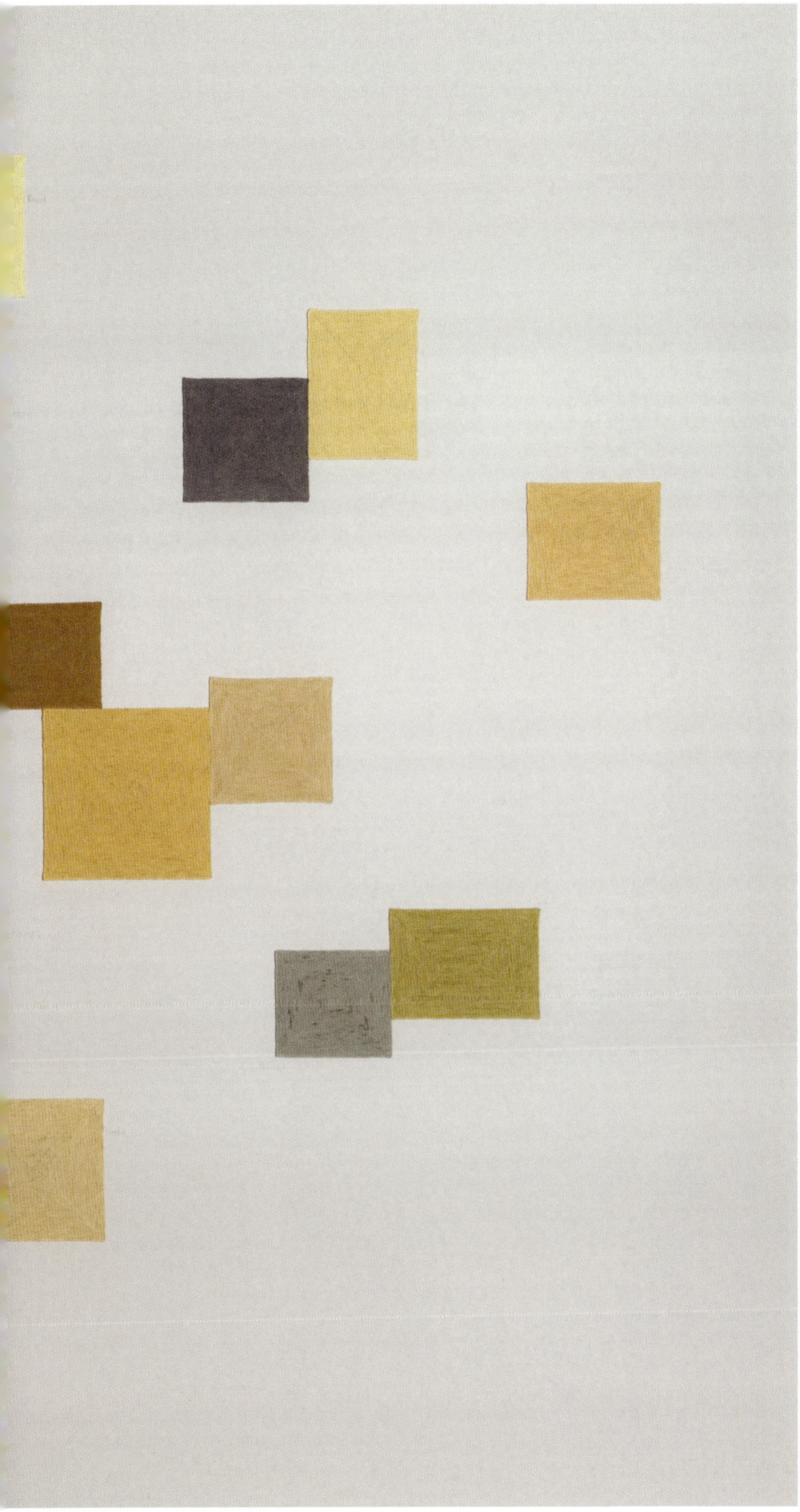

CAT. 16

Hildur Bjarnadóttir (Icelandic, 1969–). *Urban Color Palette, Charlotte*, 2010, crocheted Icelandic wool, plant dyes, 103" x 148".

Project Ten Ten Ten Commission. Gift of Wesley Mancini, the International Textile Manufacturers Association, and Berhan Nebioglu and Michael Gallis, Michael Gallis and Associates. 2010.64A-KK. © Hildur Bjarnadóttir 2010
Photo: David H. Ramsey

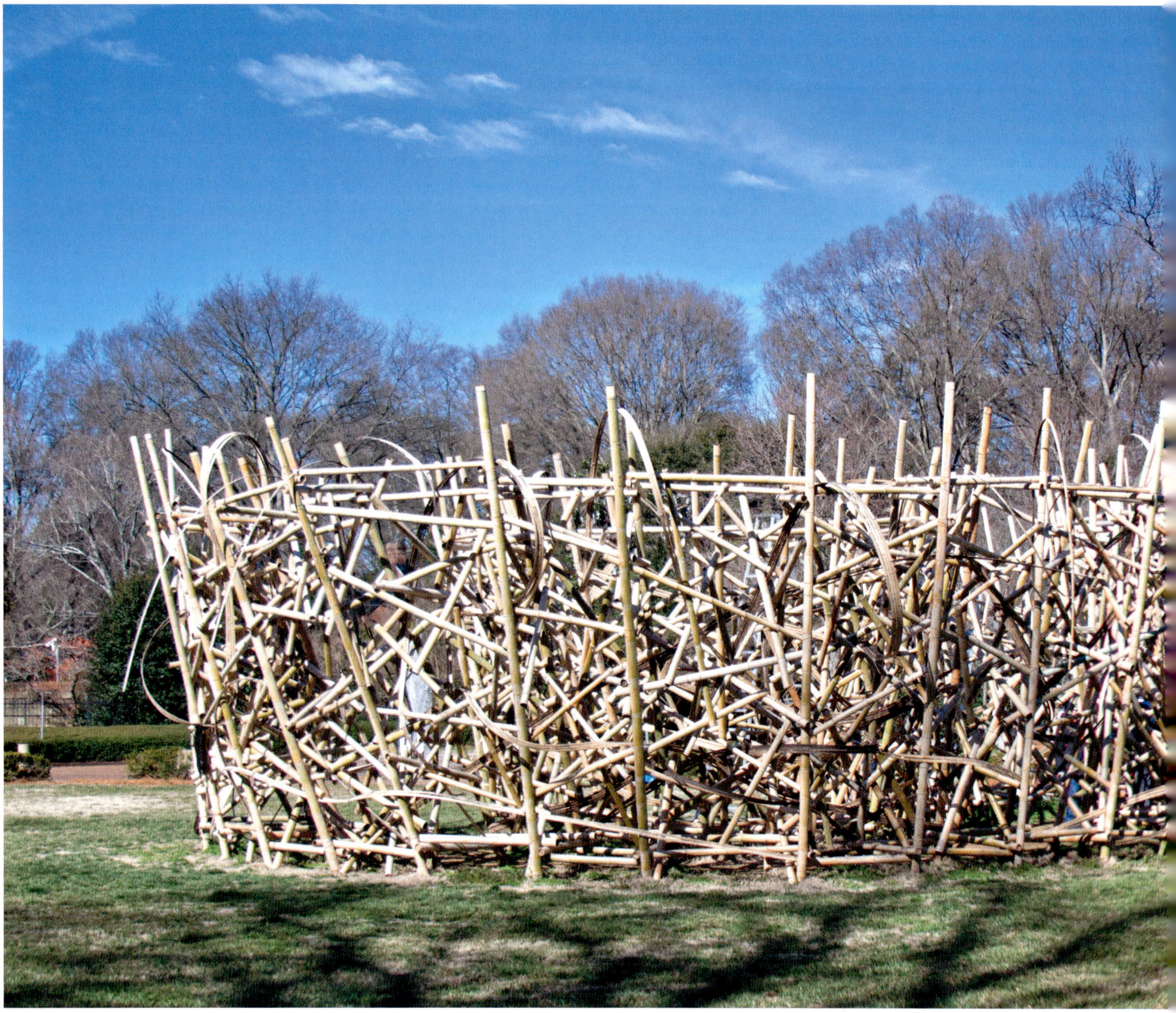

CAT. 17

Tetsunori Kawana (Japanese, 1945–). *Passage: Waterway*, 2011–12, straight and split madake bamboo, annealed metal wire, 20' x 80'.

Installation funded by the Young Affiliates of the Mint; special thanks to Sterling Magnolia Apartments, Peg Sullivan, Patrick George of Heartwood Tree Service, UNITS Portable Storage, and Ray Peavy of The Big Bamboo Company. © Tetsunori Kawana, 2011
Photo: James Martin

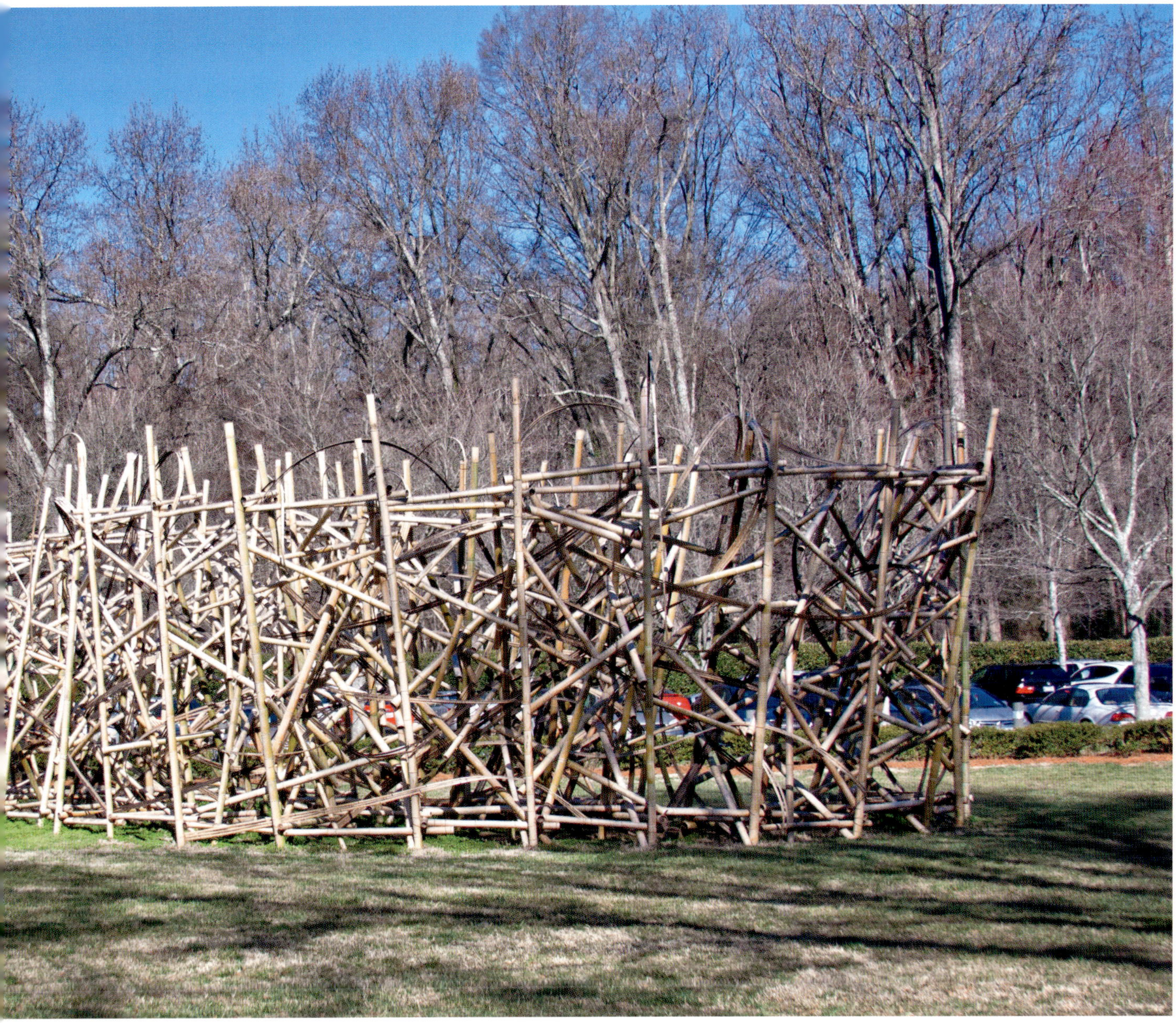

CAT . 18

Kate Malone (British, 1959–).
***Mr. and Mrs. Tutti Atomic*,**
2012, molded and hand-built stoneware, glaze, 32" x 24.125" x 25" (Mr.); 25" x 25.5" x 25" (Mrs.).

Project Ten Ten Ten Commission. Museum Purchase: Founders' Circle 2011 Annual Cause, with additional funds provided by various donors. 2012.13.1-2. © Kate Malone, 2012
Photo: Andrew Smart

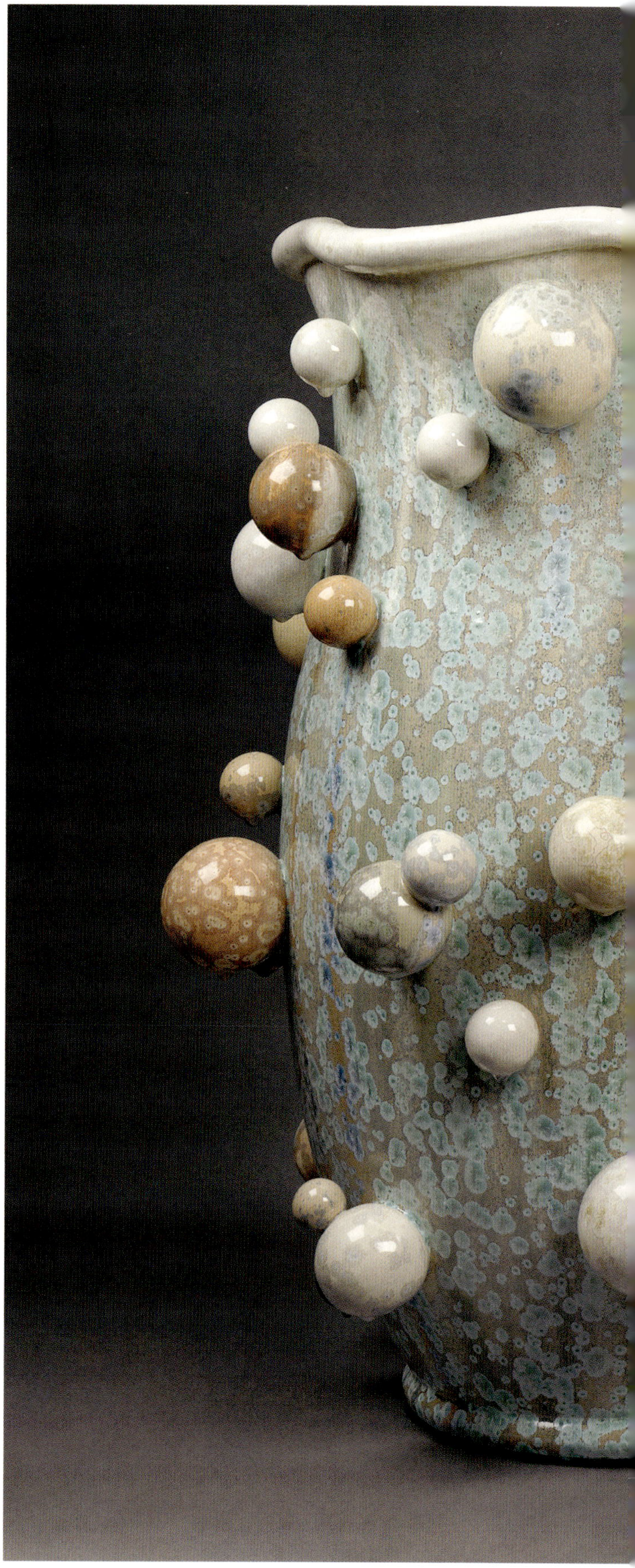

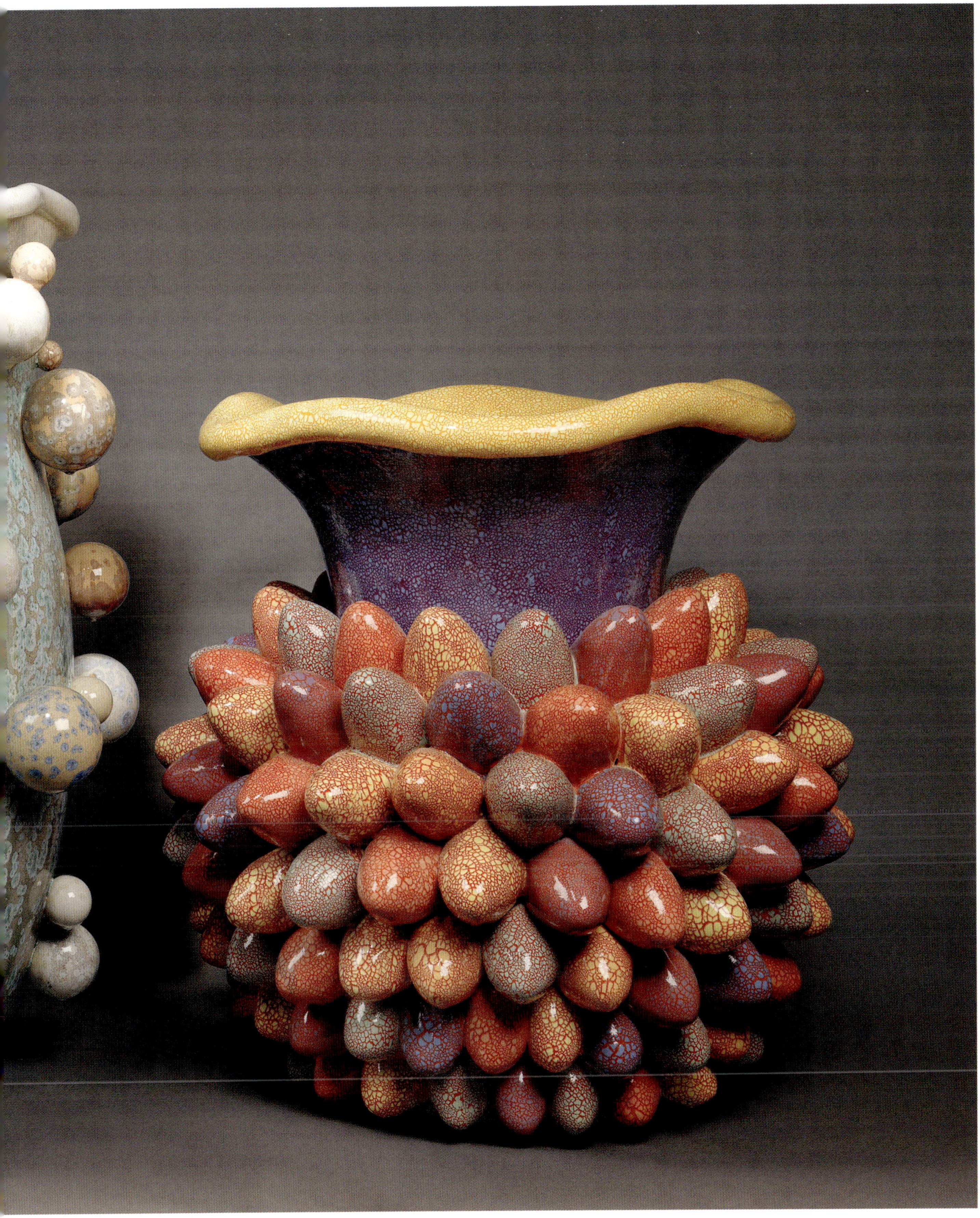

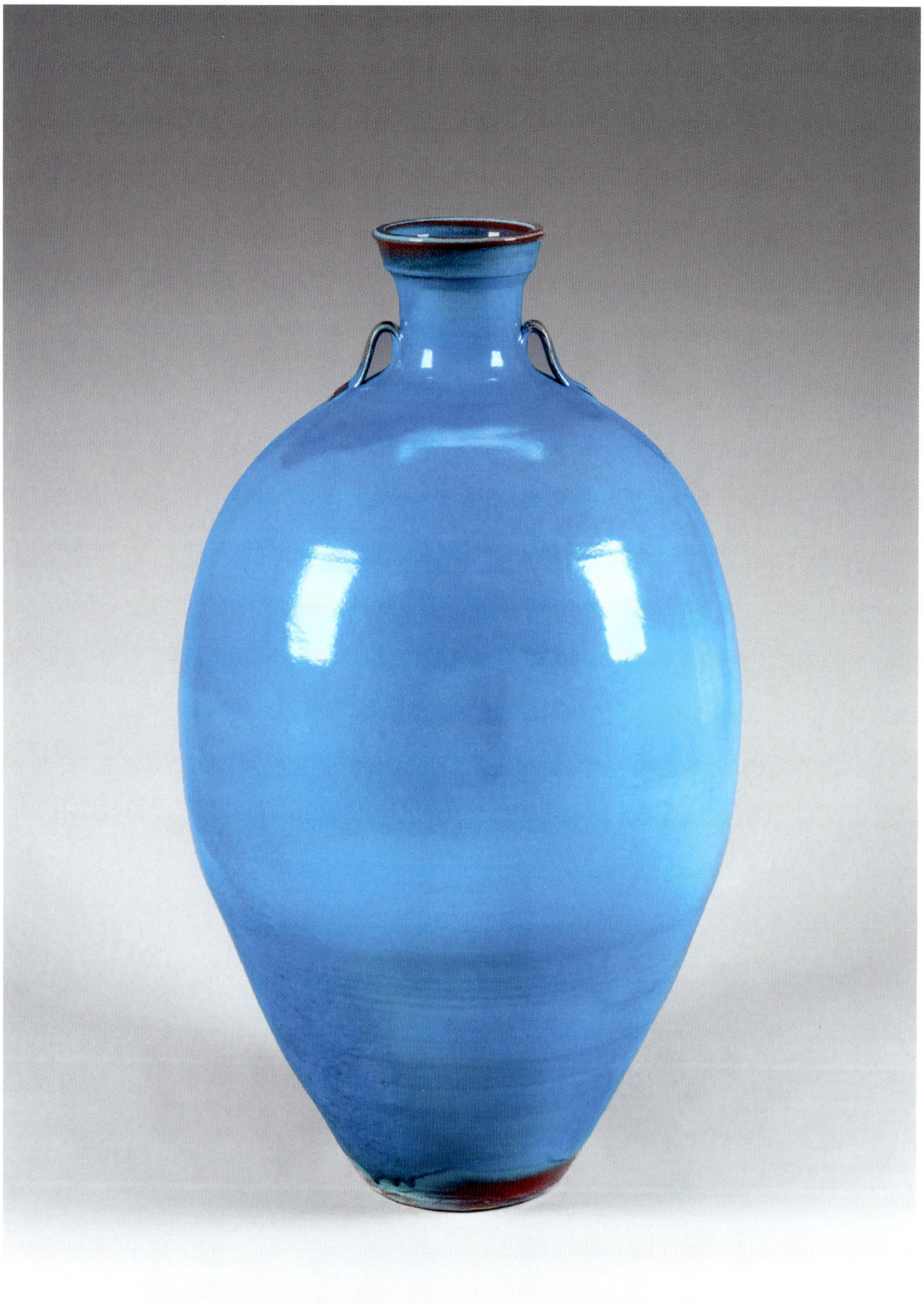

CAT. 19

Ben Owen III (American, 1968–).
***MiSe Vase*, 2016, glazed stoneware, 41" x 24".**

Daisy Wade Bridges Purchase Prize from the 2016 Potters Market Invitational, given by the Delhom Service League. 2016.38.1
Photo: Keara Reburn

CAT. 20

Michael Eden (English, 1955–).
***Imari I*, 2014, 3D-printed nylon, mineral, 11.75" x 9.5" x 8.625".**

Museum Purchase: Founders' Circle Gala Annual Cause 2015. 2015.16.1A-B.
© Michael Eden, 2014

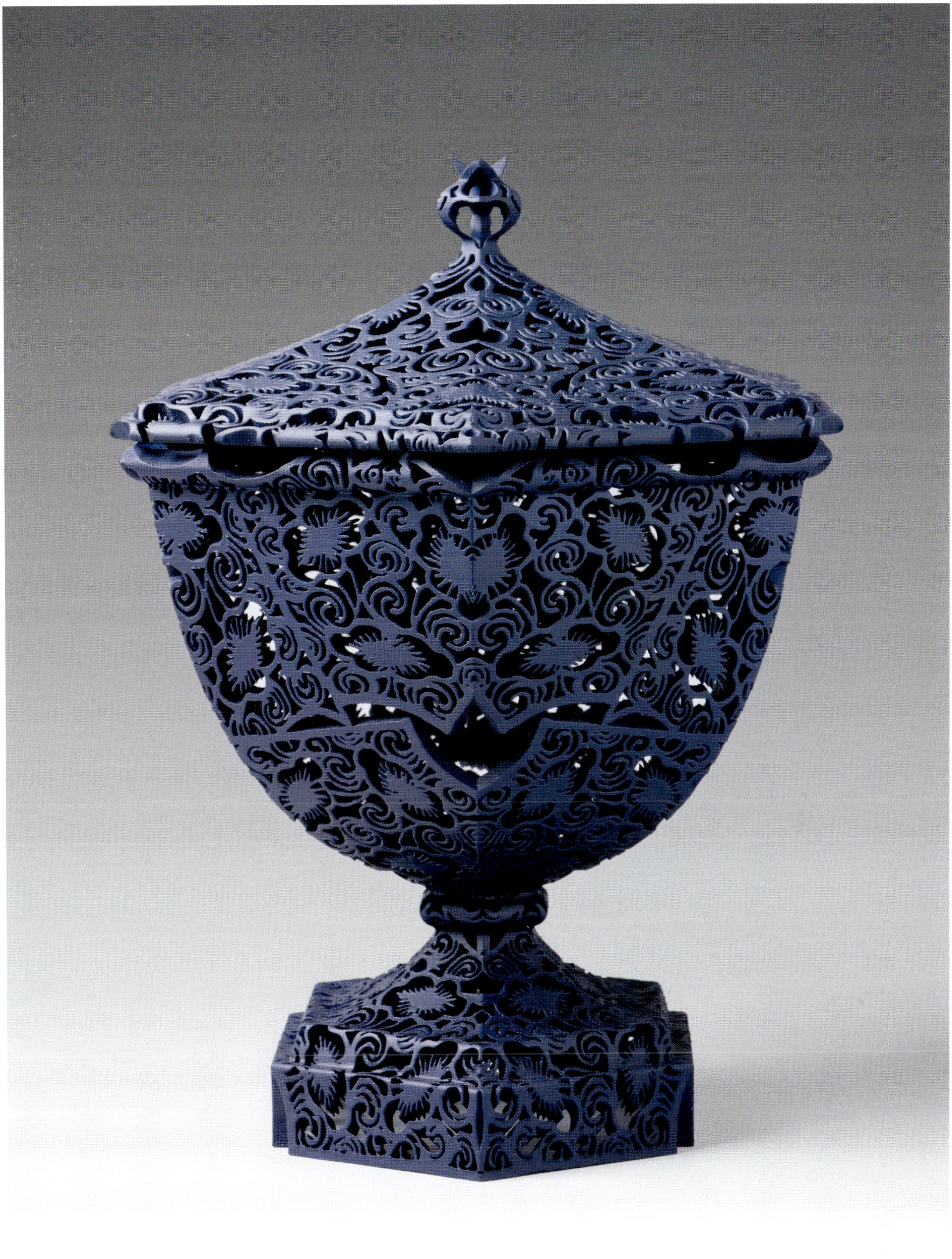

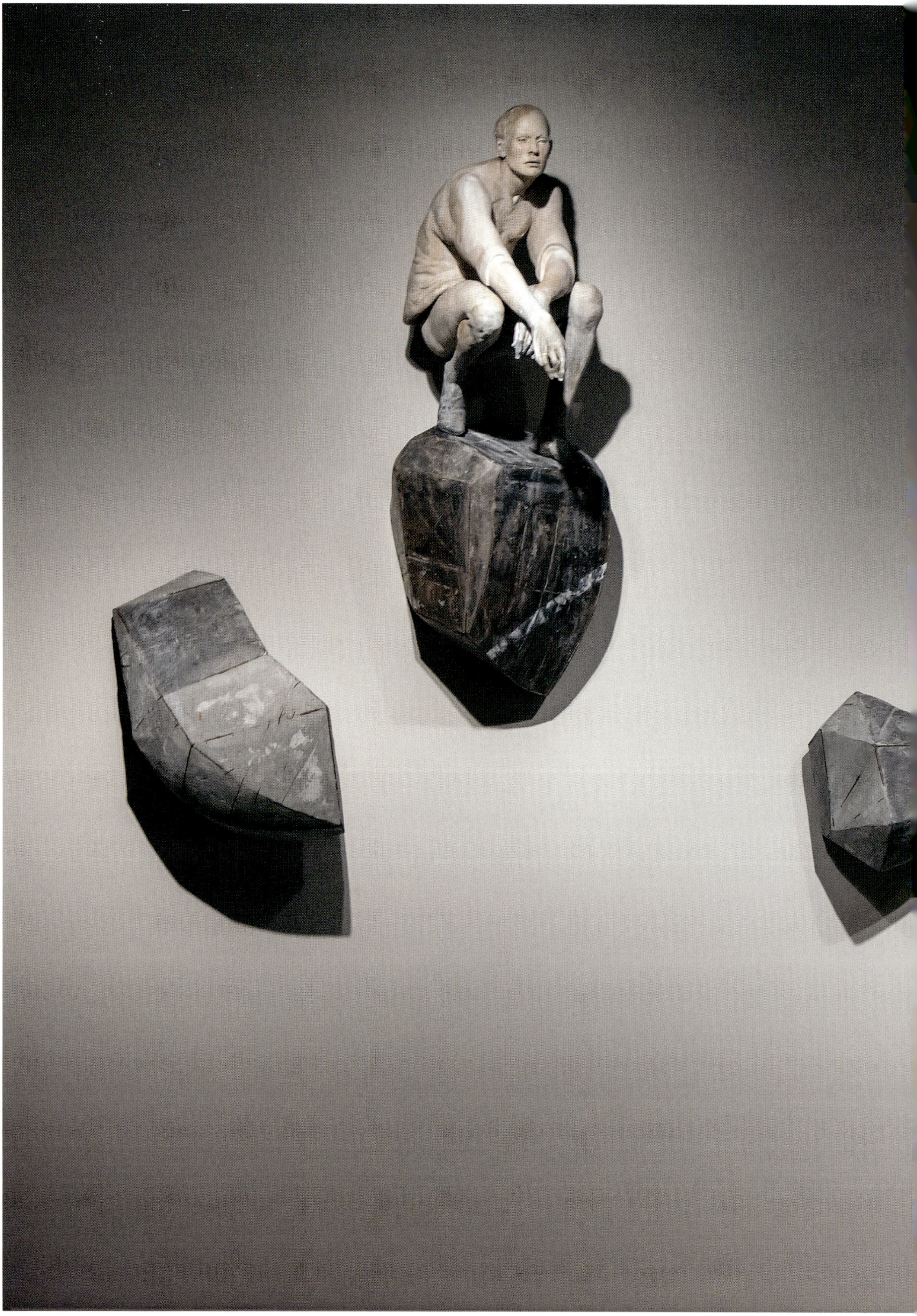

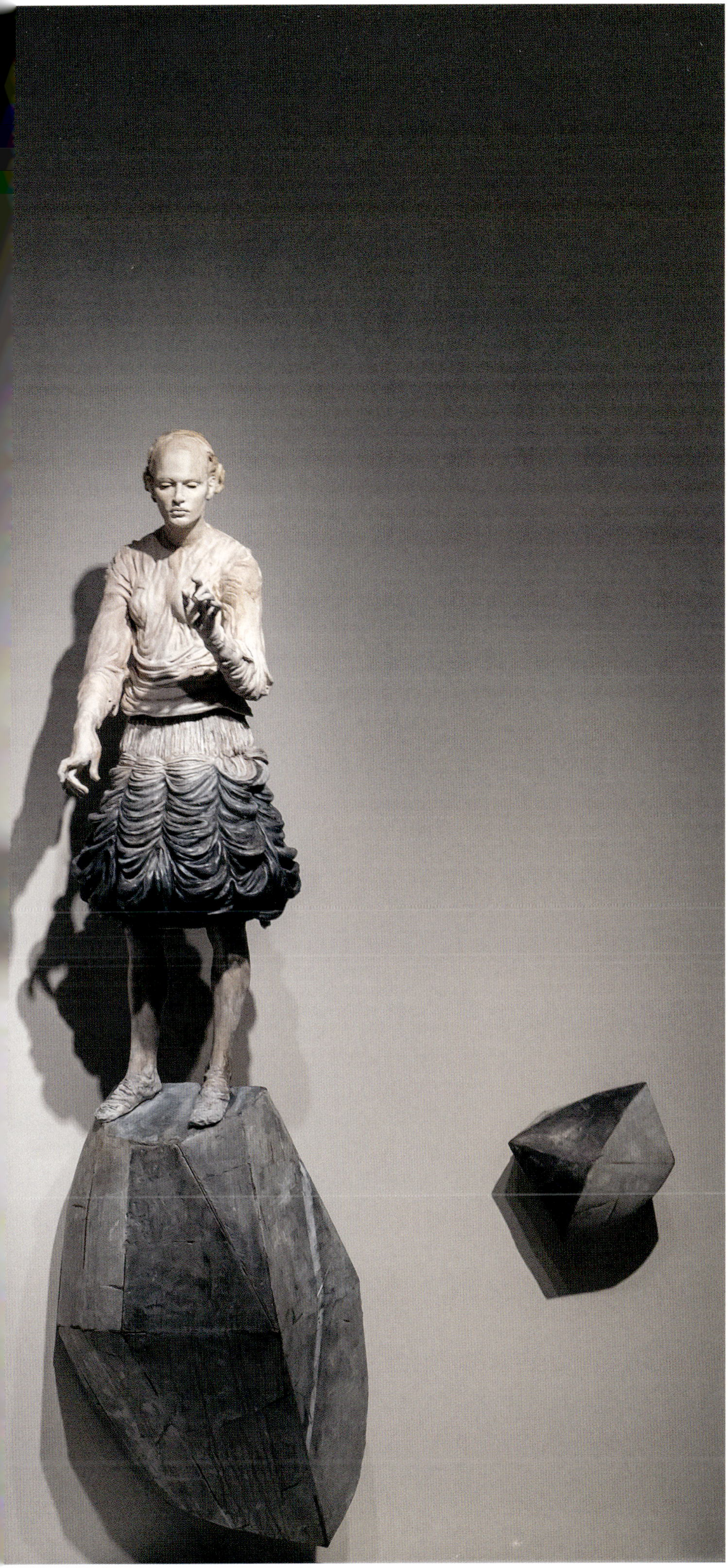

CAT. 21

Cristina Córdova (Puerto Rican [active United States], 1977–). *Preludios y Partidas*, 2012, ceramic, concrete, steel, resin, 129.5" x 180" x 36".

Project Ten Ten Ten Commission. Museum Purchase: Funds provided by Laura and Michael Grace, Donna and Al De Molina, Lorne Lassiter and Gary Ferraro, and Yvonne and Richard McCracken. 2014.30A-J.

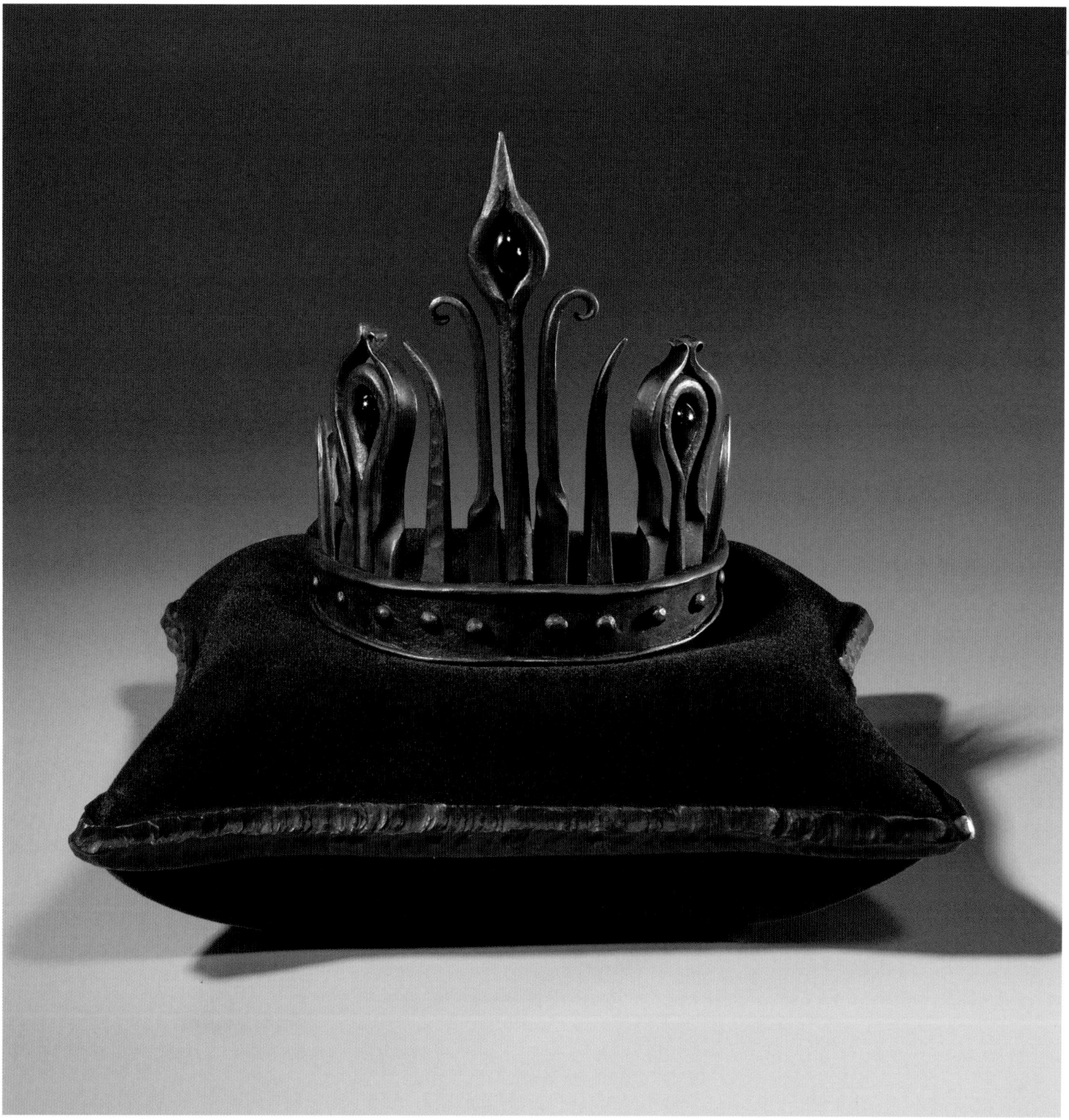

CAT. 22

Elizabeth Brim (American, 1951–).
***A Dark Tale*, 2011, forged and fabricated steel, flocked fiber, glass, 11" x 12" x 11.25".**

Gift of Founders' Circle, Ltd. in loving memory of Edward Kindall Jones. 2011.47A-B
Photo: Mitchell Kearney

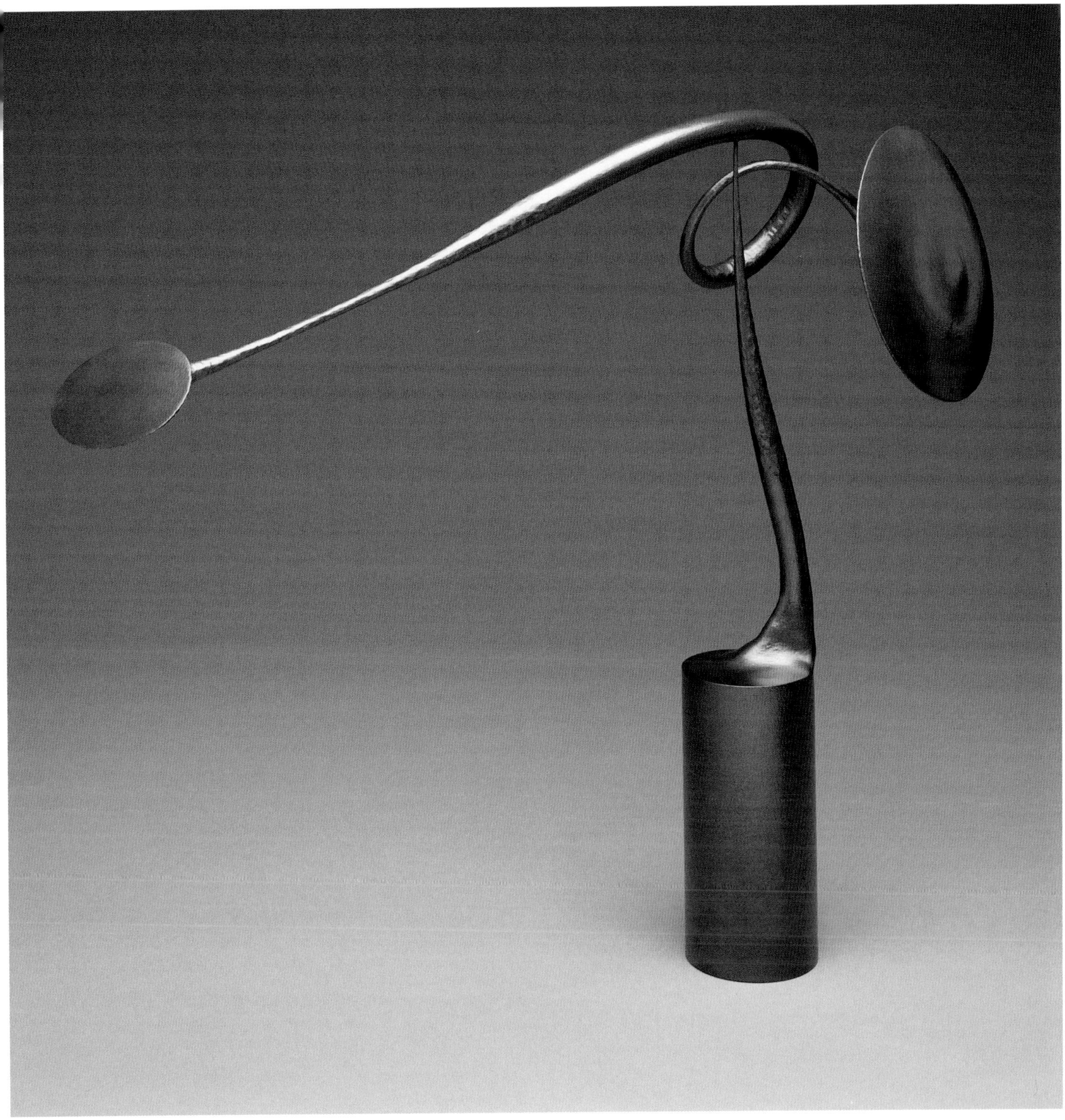

CAT. 23

Brent Kington (American, 1934–2013). *Weathervane*, 1981, forged and oxyacetelene gas-welded mild steel, paint, 43" x 25" x 32".

Museum Purchase: Funds provided by Greg Parker and Randy Dickerson. 1999.125A-B. © L. Brent Kington 1981

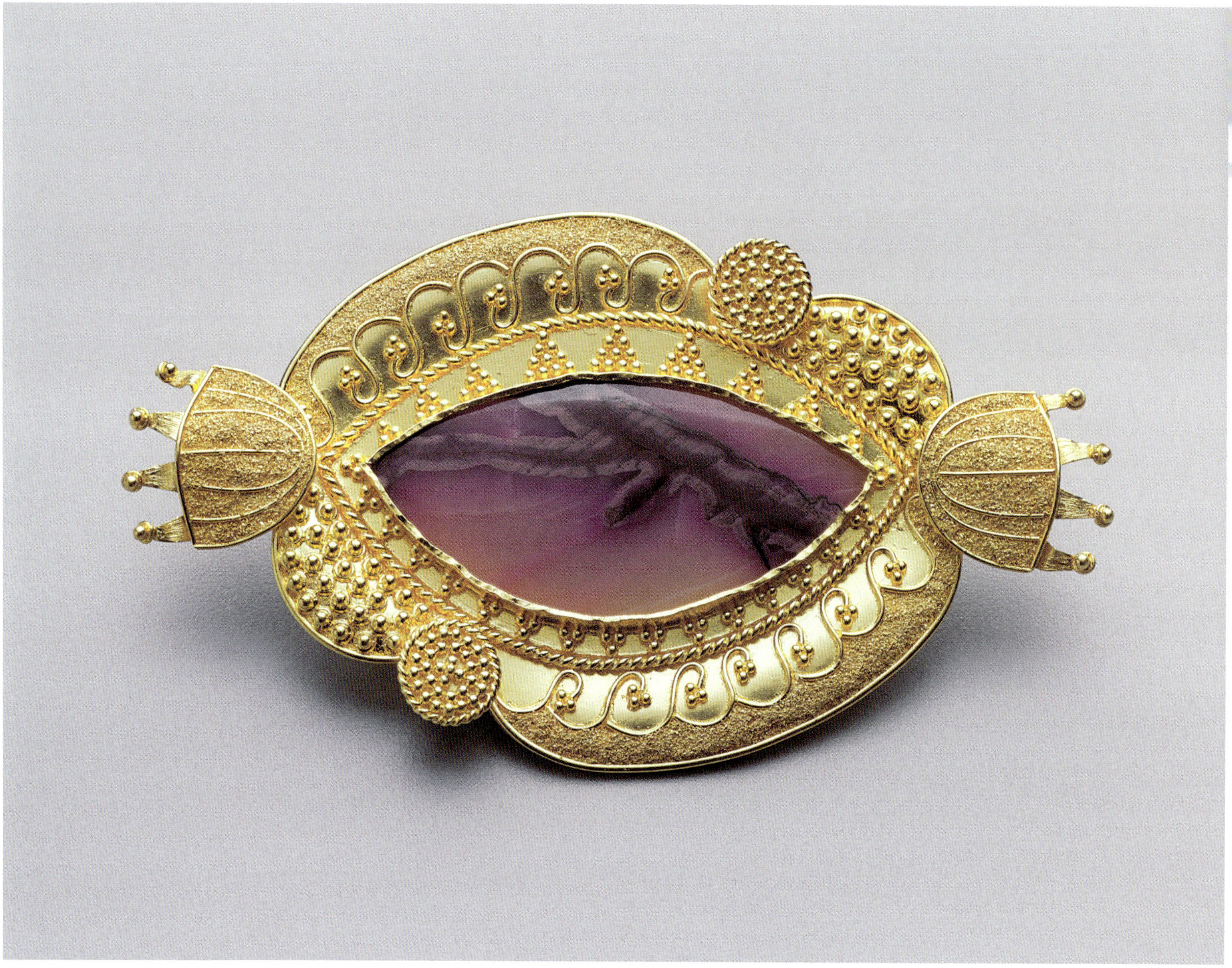

CAT. 24

Douglas Harling (American, 1959–). *Vishnu Dreams*, 1998, granulated 22-karat gold, 14-karat gold, sugilite stone, 2.75" x 3.75" x .25".

Museum Purchase: Funds provided by Sandy Berlin and Les Kooyman. 1999.112.

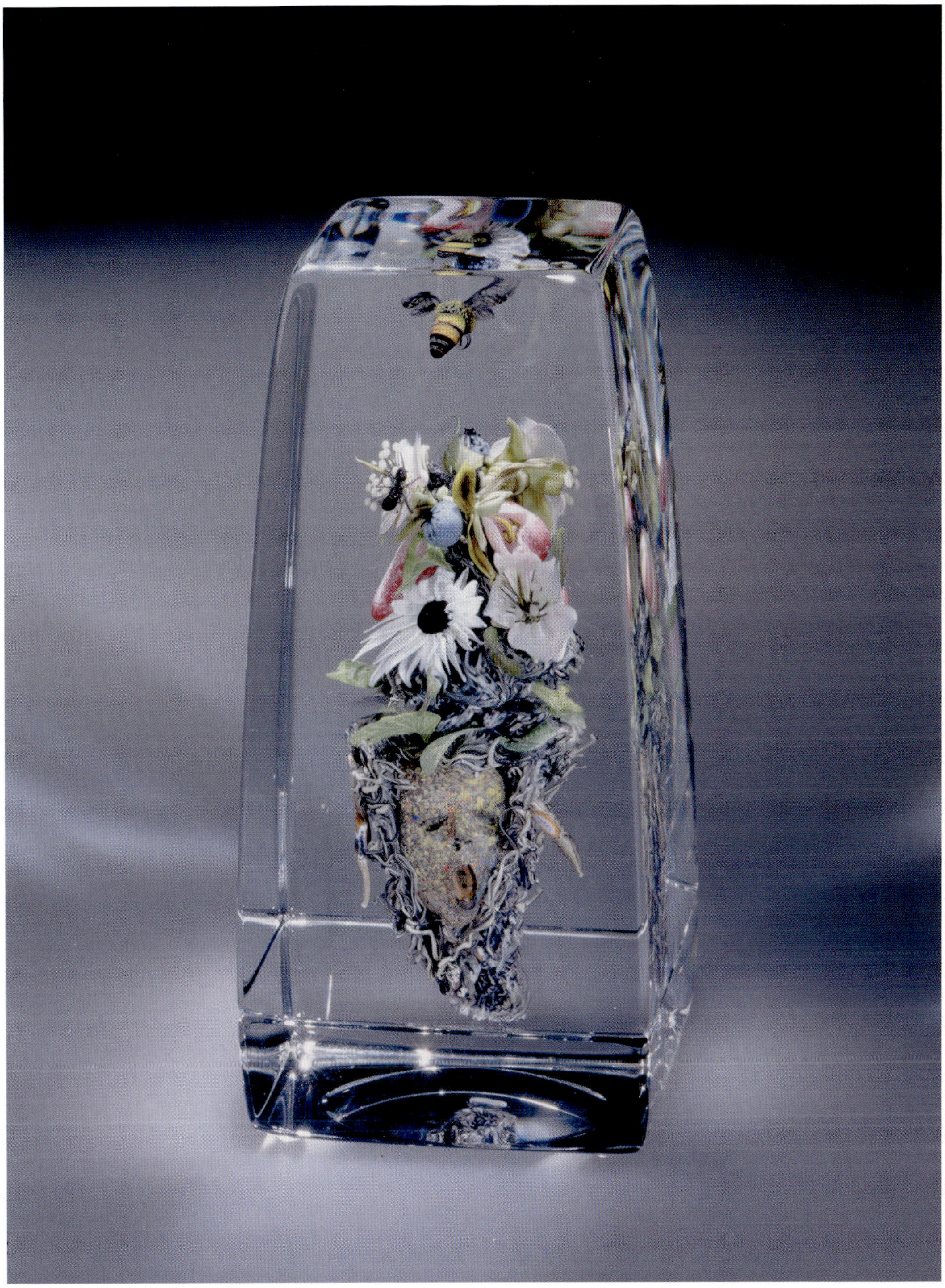

CAT. 25

Paul Stankard (American, 1943–).
Carolina Bouquet Botanical, 2001,
flame-worked, hot-worked, kiln-cast,
encased, enameled, and assembled
glass, 5.25" x 2.5" x 2.5".
Gift of the Charlotte Garden Club. 2001.67

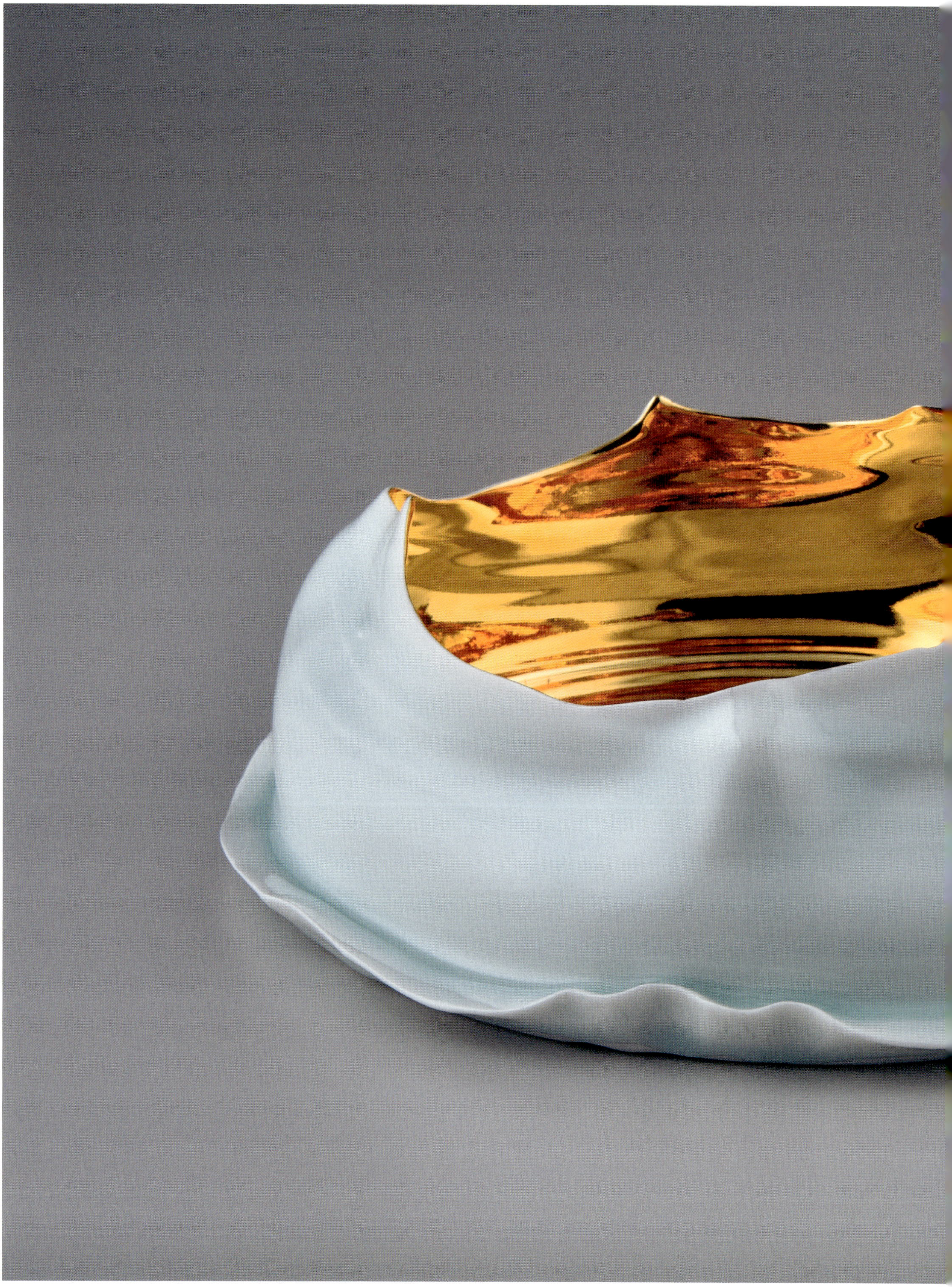

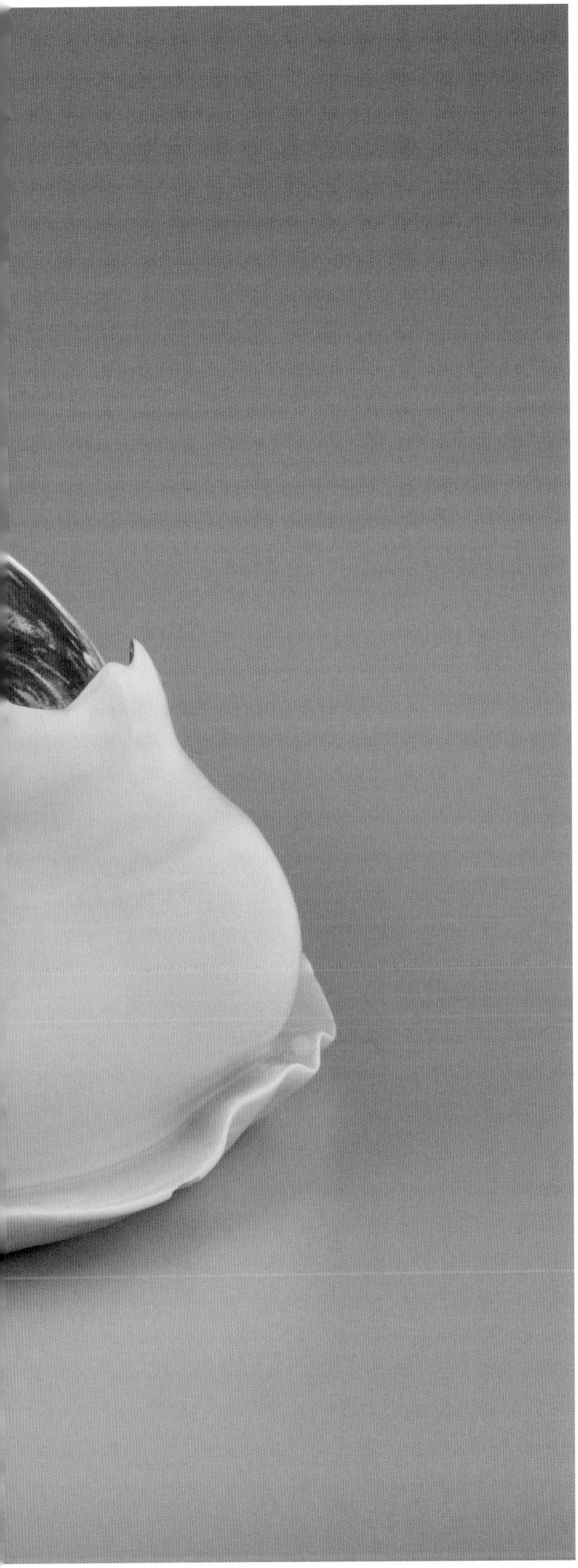

CAT. 26

Takeshi Yasuda (Japanese [active in Great Britain], 1943–). *Qingbai Celadon Bowl with Golden Interior*, 2018, wheel-thrown and glazed porcelain, colloidal gold, 5" x 12.5" x 11.125".

Museum Purchase: Funds provided by Ann and Michael Tarwater in honor of Annie Carlano. 2019.75

Photo: Brandon Scott

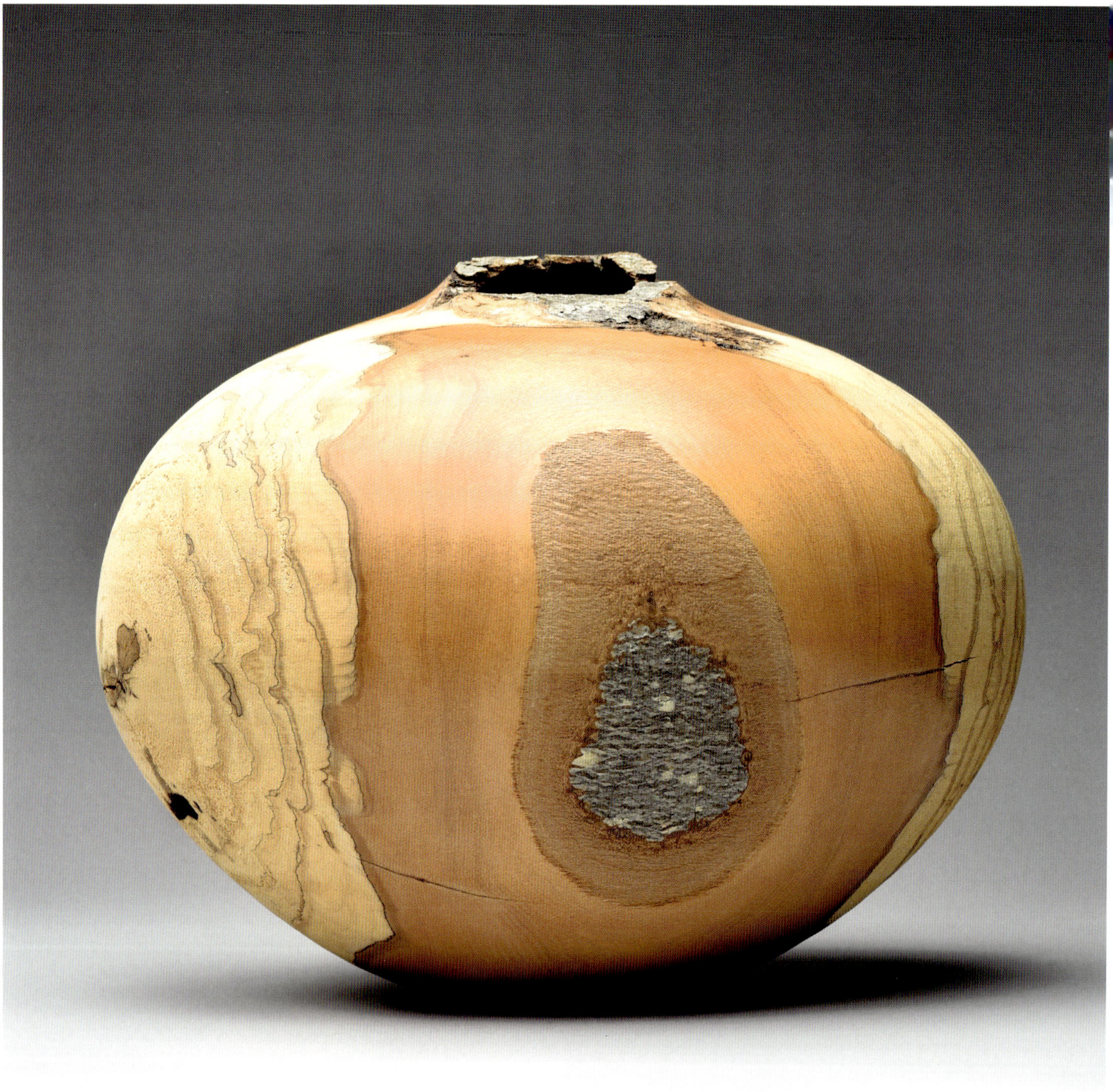

CAT. 27

David Ellsworth (American, 1944–).
***Untitled Vessel*, 1987, lathe-turned beech wood, 14" x 19" x 19".**
Gift of Jane and Arthur Mason. 1998.119.1.

Photo: Brandon Scott

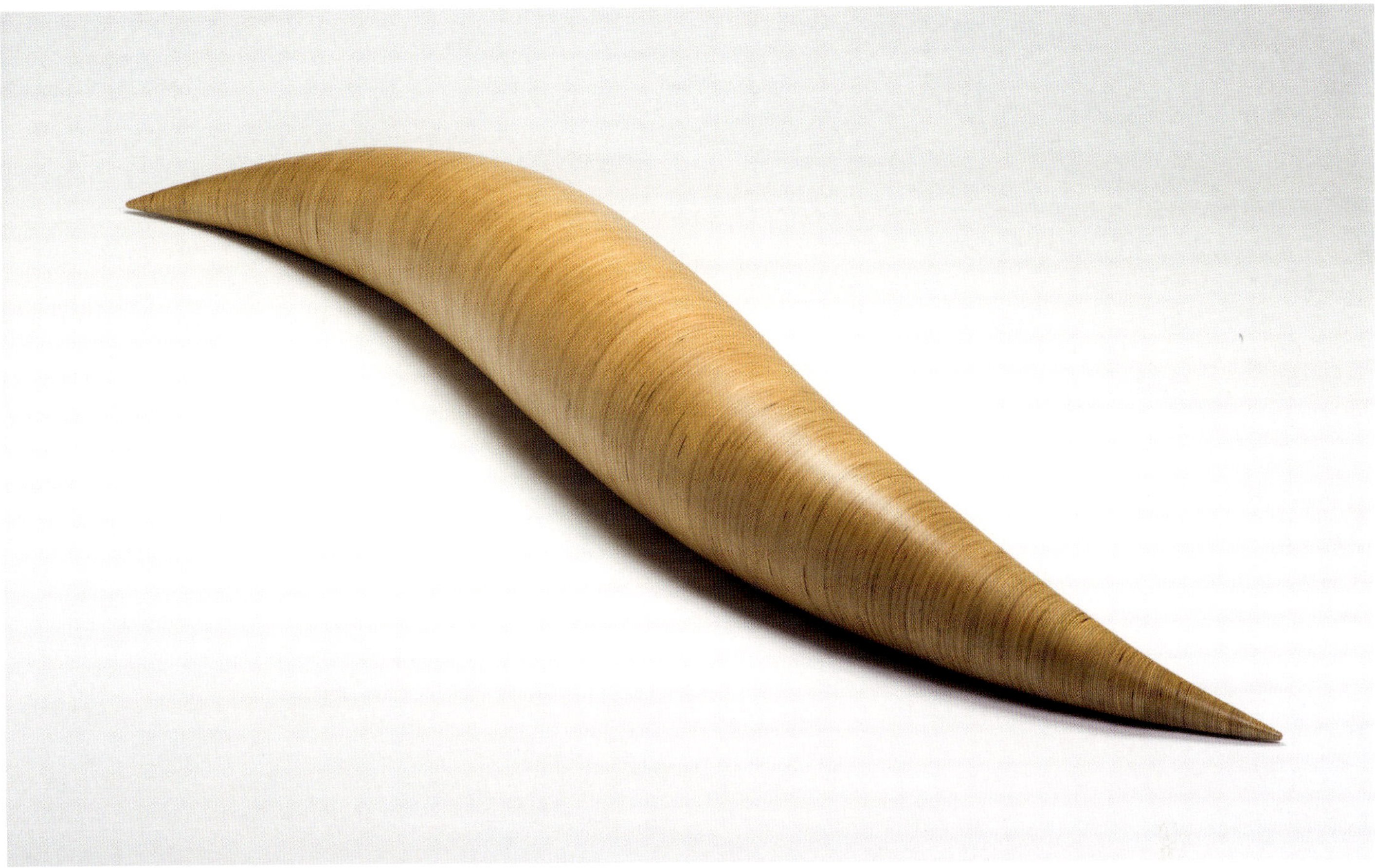

CAT. 28

Donald Fortescue (Australian, 1957–). *Pike Basking*, 2000–01, laminated and turned Finnish birch wood, lacquer, 12" x 102.5" x 21".

Museum Purchase: Funds provided by Marc and Diane Grainer and Ronald and Anita Wornick. 2003.29. © Donald Fortescue 2003
Photo: David H. Ramsey

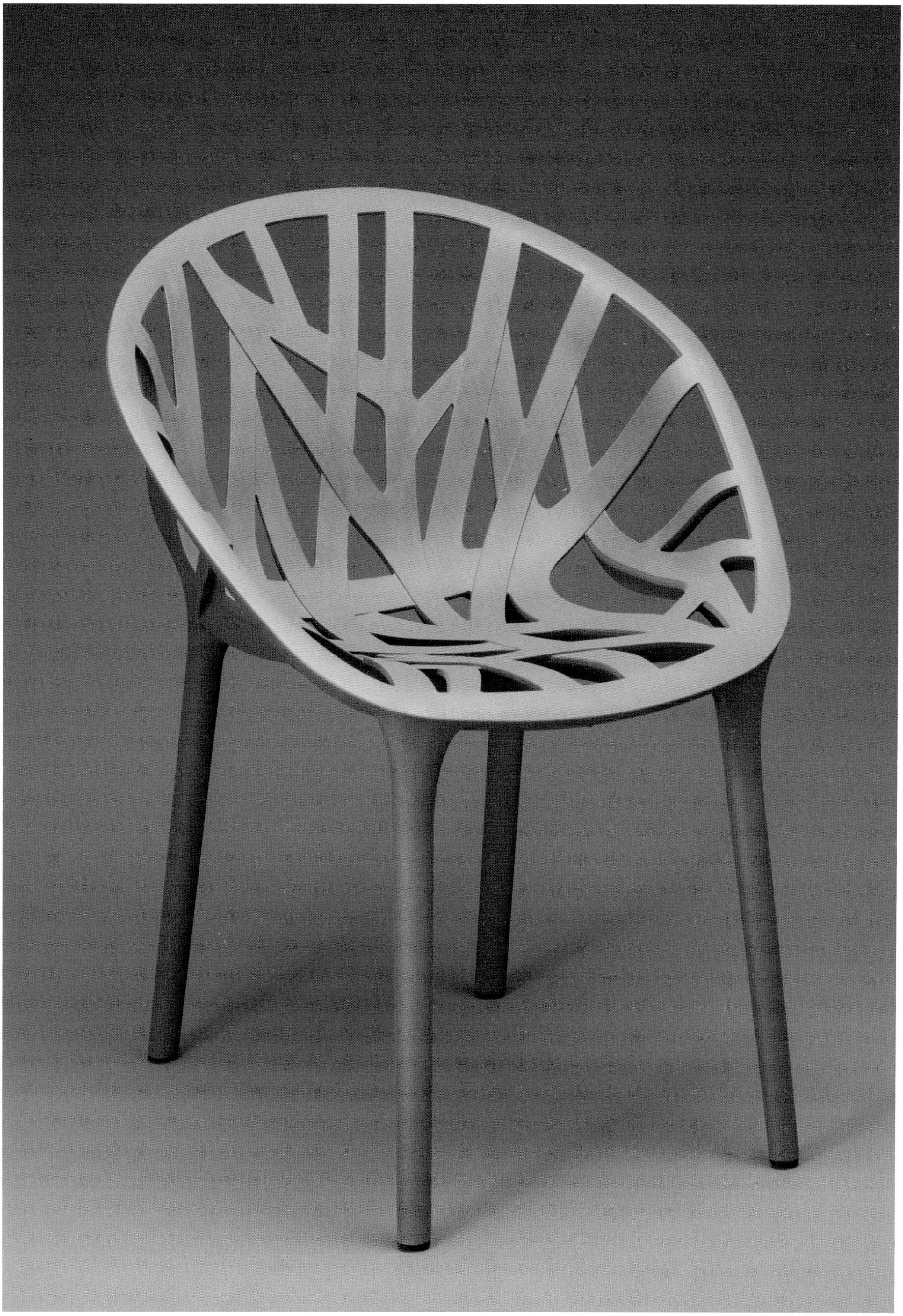

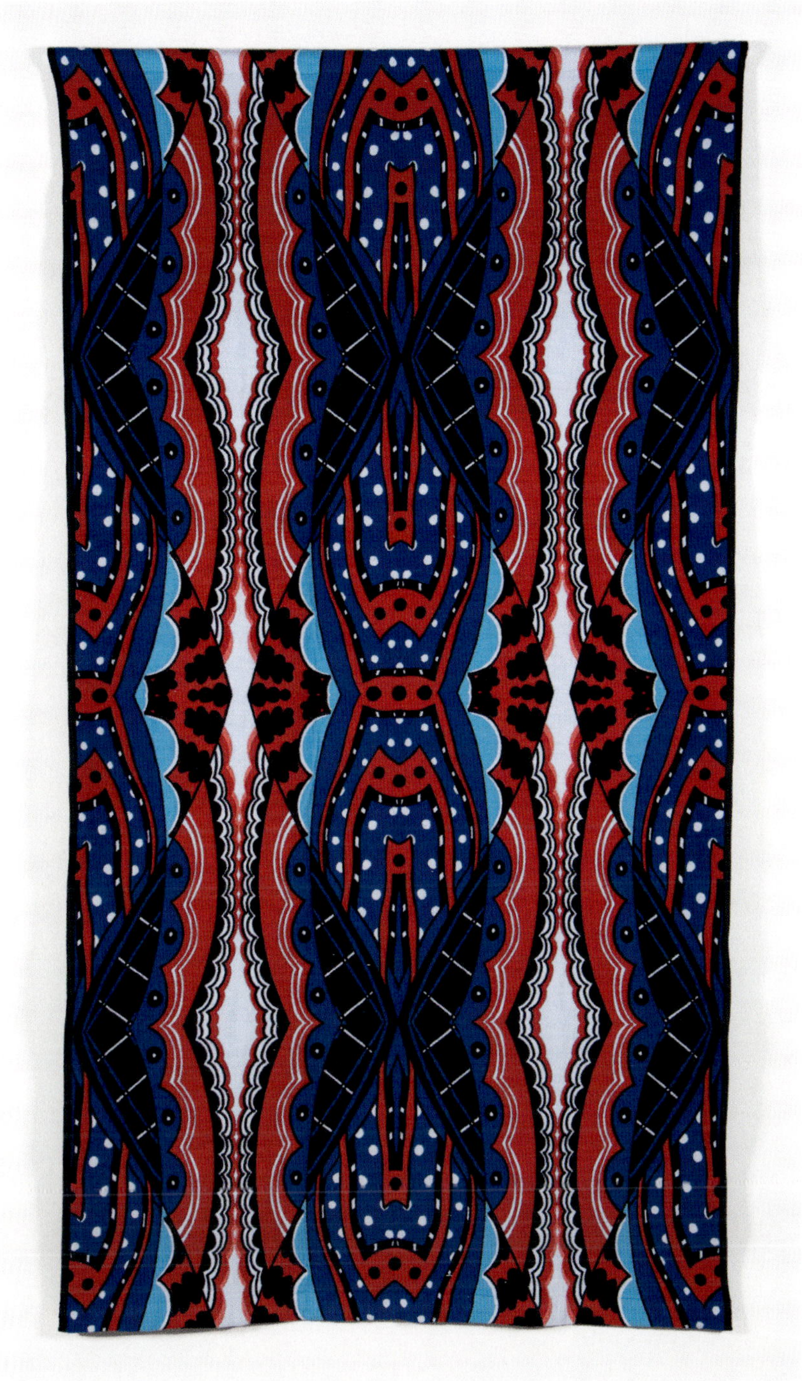

CAT. 29

Ronan Bouroullec (French, 1971–). Erwan Bouroullec (French, 1976–). Vitra, Inc. (1950–). *Vegetal Chair*, 2008, injection-molded and dyed plastic, 32" x 23.75" x 21.75".

Gift of Vitra. 2010.21
Photo: Brandon Scott

CAT. 30

Christie van der Haak (Dutch, 1950–), *Edda*, 2008–16, Jacquard-woven acrylic and cotton, 113.625" x 62.25".

Gift of Ashley and Scott Mattei. 2016.49
Photo: Brandon Scott

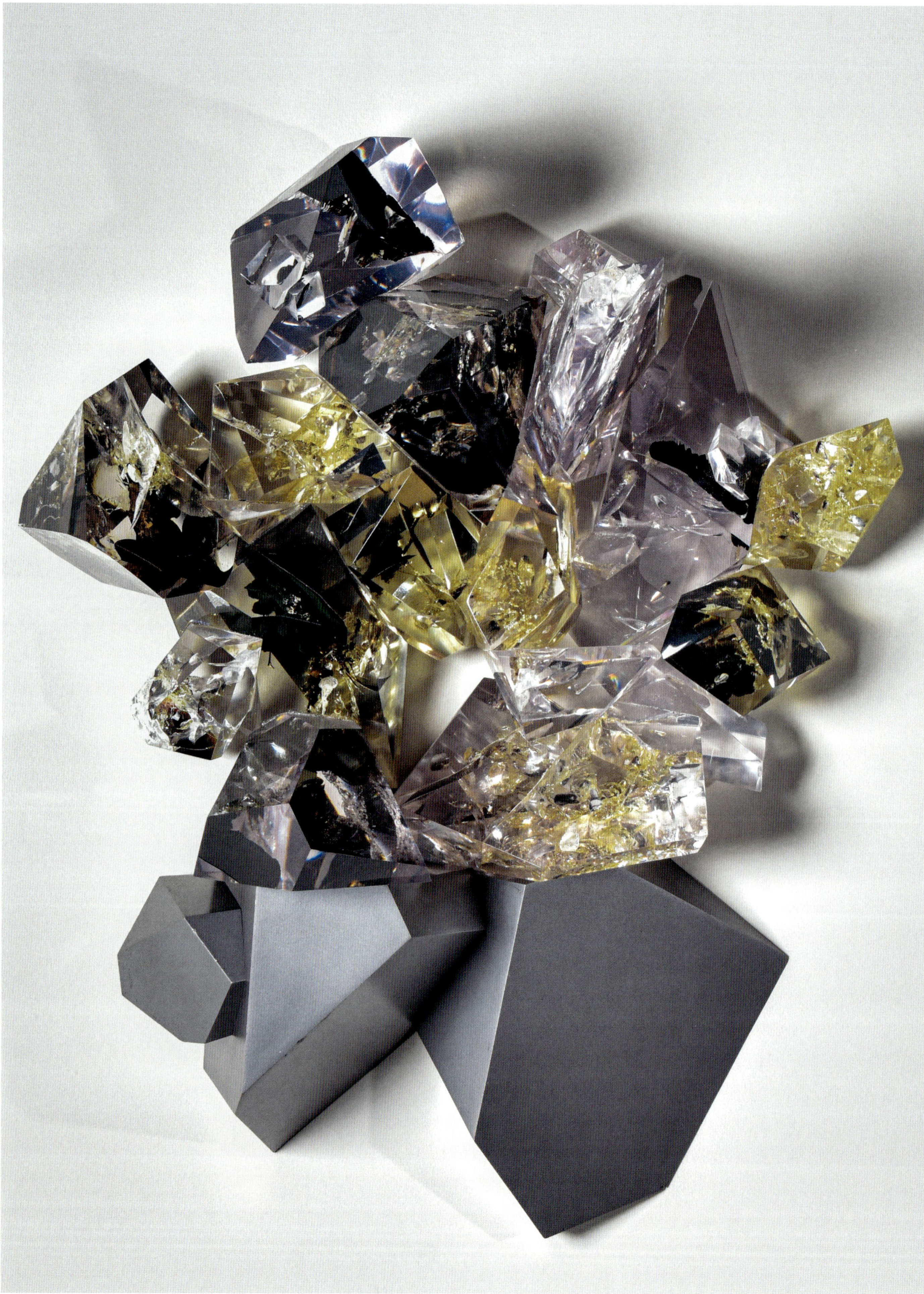

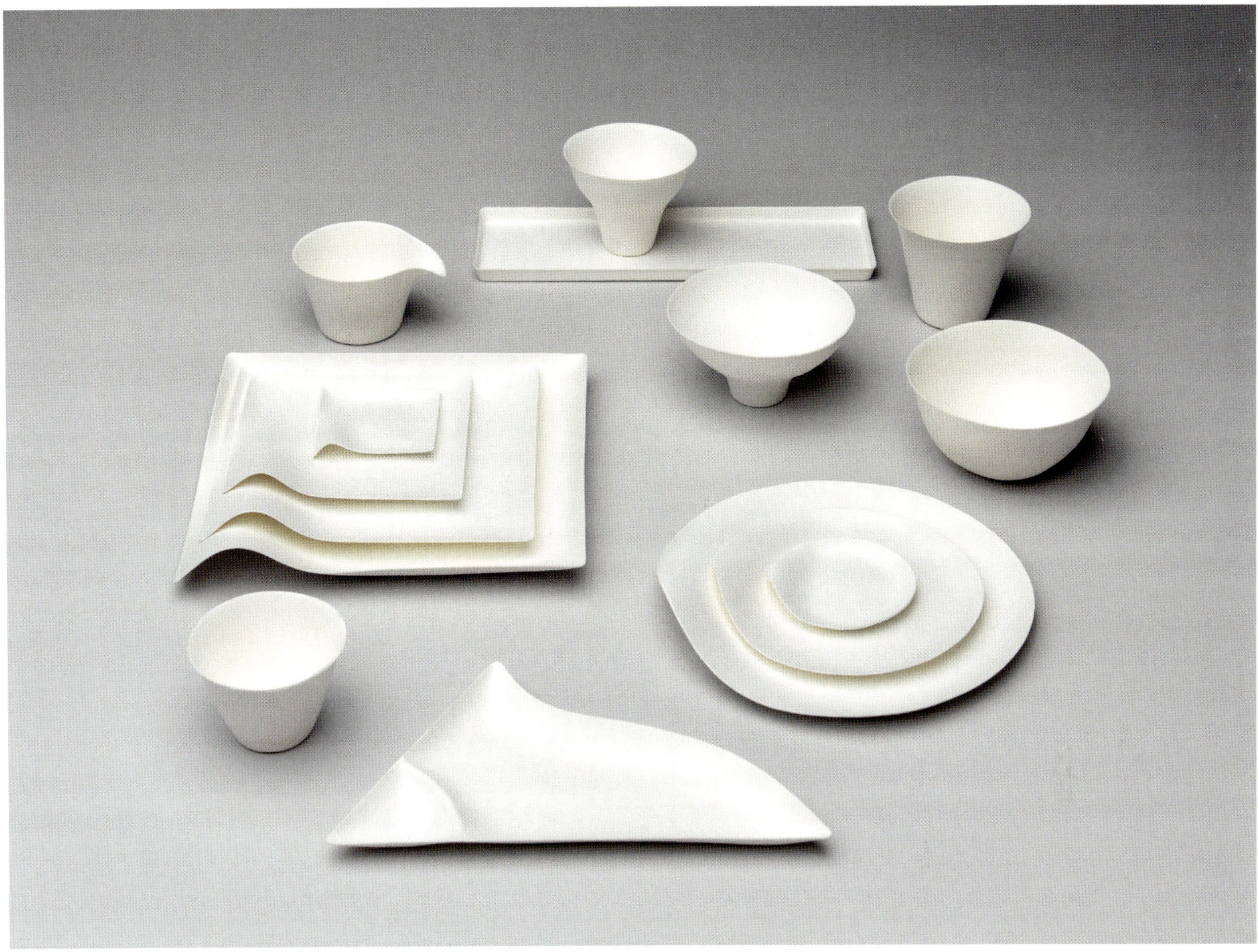

CAT. 31

Tom Price (British, 1973–). *Synthesis X*, 2016, resin, tar, steel, LEDs, 35.875" x 26" x 13".

Gift of Laura B. and Michael F. Grace. 2016.52A-D

Photo: Brandon Scott

CAT. 32

Shinichiro Ogata (Japanese, 1969–). SIMPLICITY Co., Ltd. WASARA, Ltd. (Tokyo, Japan, 2008–). ***WASARA Biodegradable Tableware***, 2011, sugar cane fiber, bamboo, reed pulp, largest: 0.875" x 9.62" x 9.62"; smallest: 0.125" x 3.125" x 3.125.

Gift of Branch Projects, Inc. 2012.59.1-15

Photo: Brandon Scott

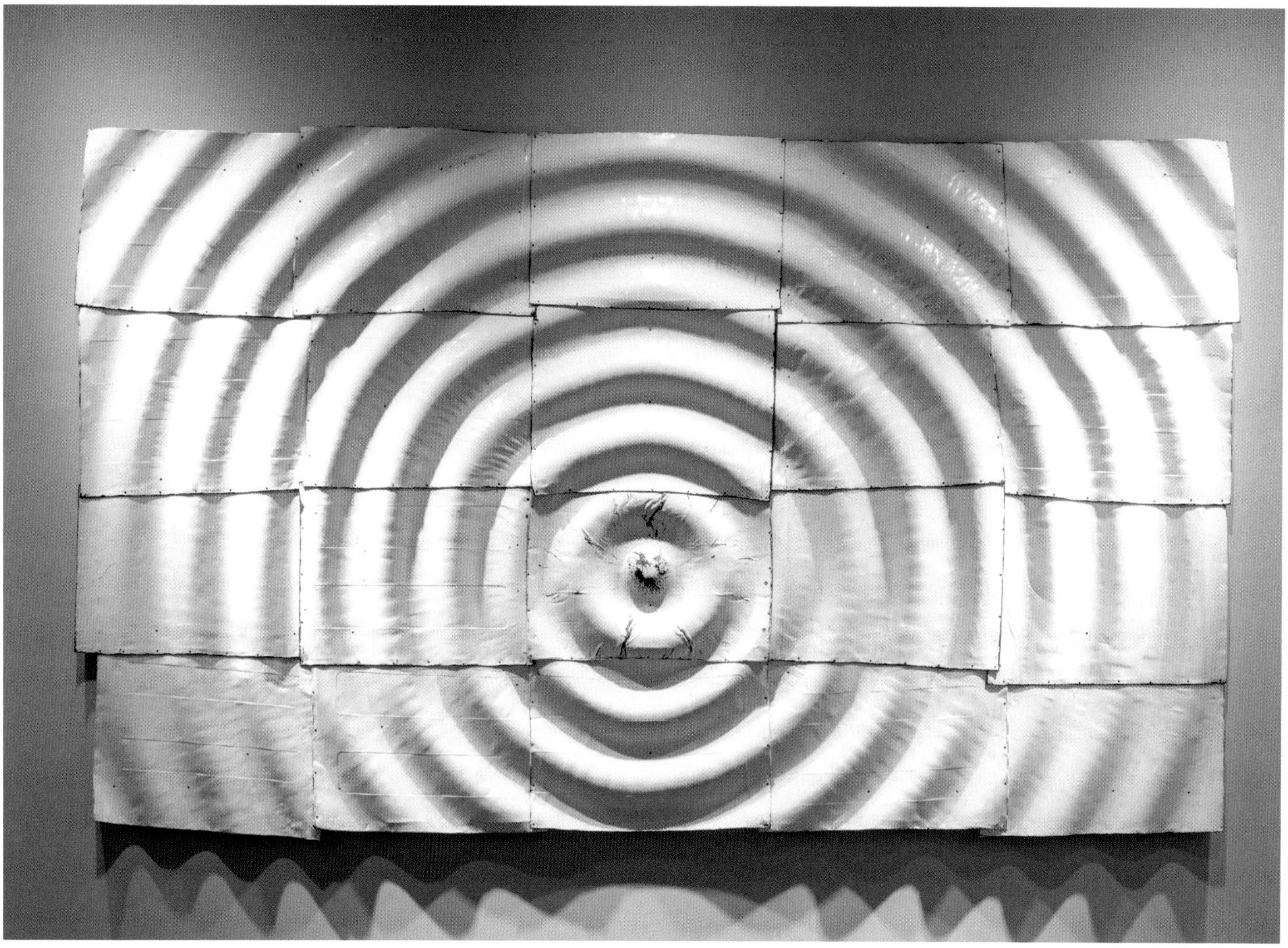

CAT. 33

Hoss Haley (American, 1961–).
***White Ripple*, 2013, embossed metal, 89" x 149".**

Museum Purchase: Funds provided by Windgate Charitable Foundation. 2013.59.
© 2013 Hoss Haley
Photo: Brandon Scott

CAT. 34

Chad Alice Hagen (American, 1949–).
***Wall One: Akai*, 1993, hand-dyed merino wool felt, plastic buttons, thread, muslin, 92" x 73".**

Museum Purchase: Funds provided by Judith Emken, Robert Emken, and Janice Emken Mullin in memory of Grace H. Emken. 1999.3

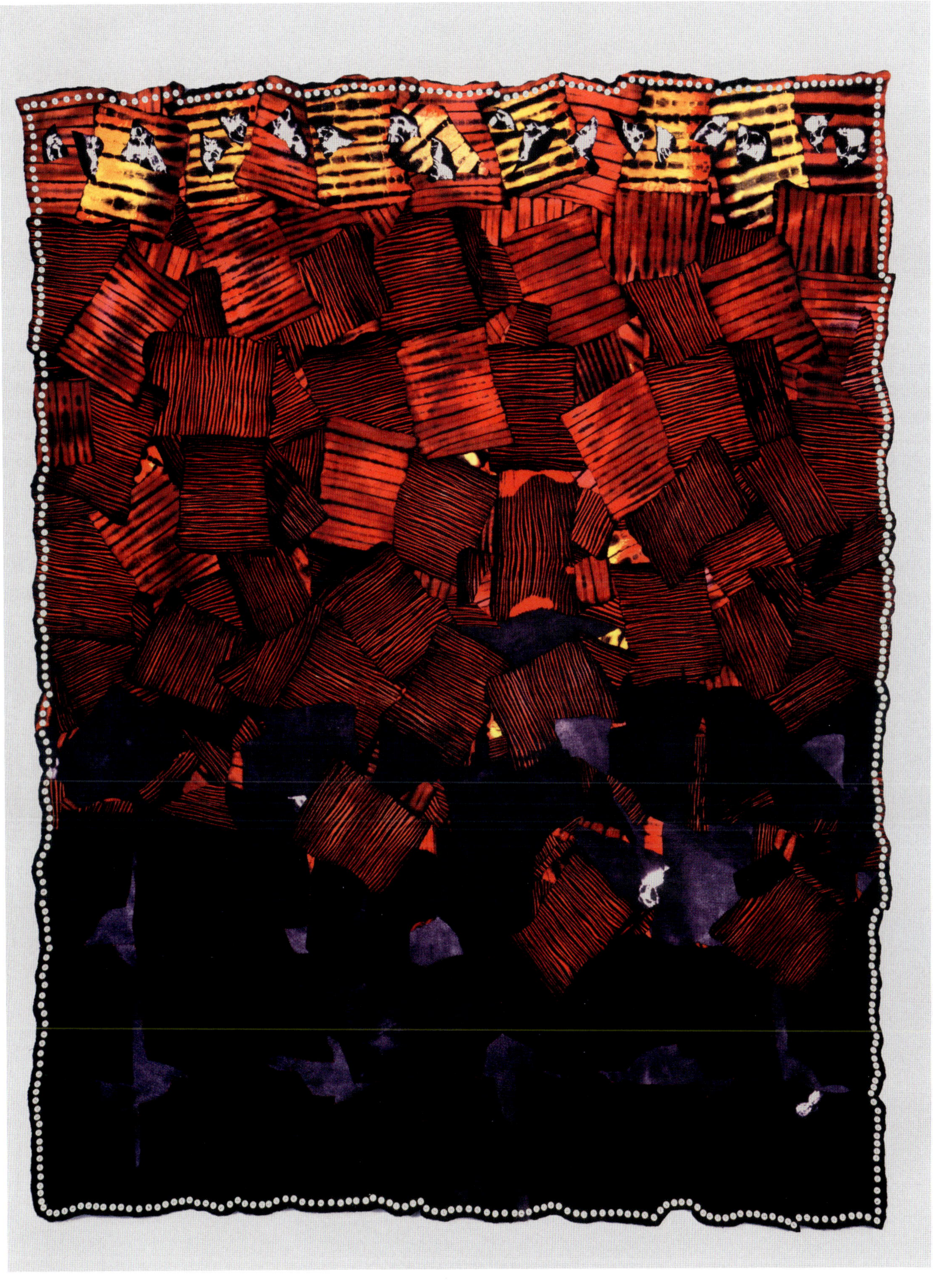

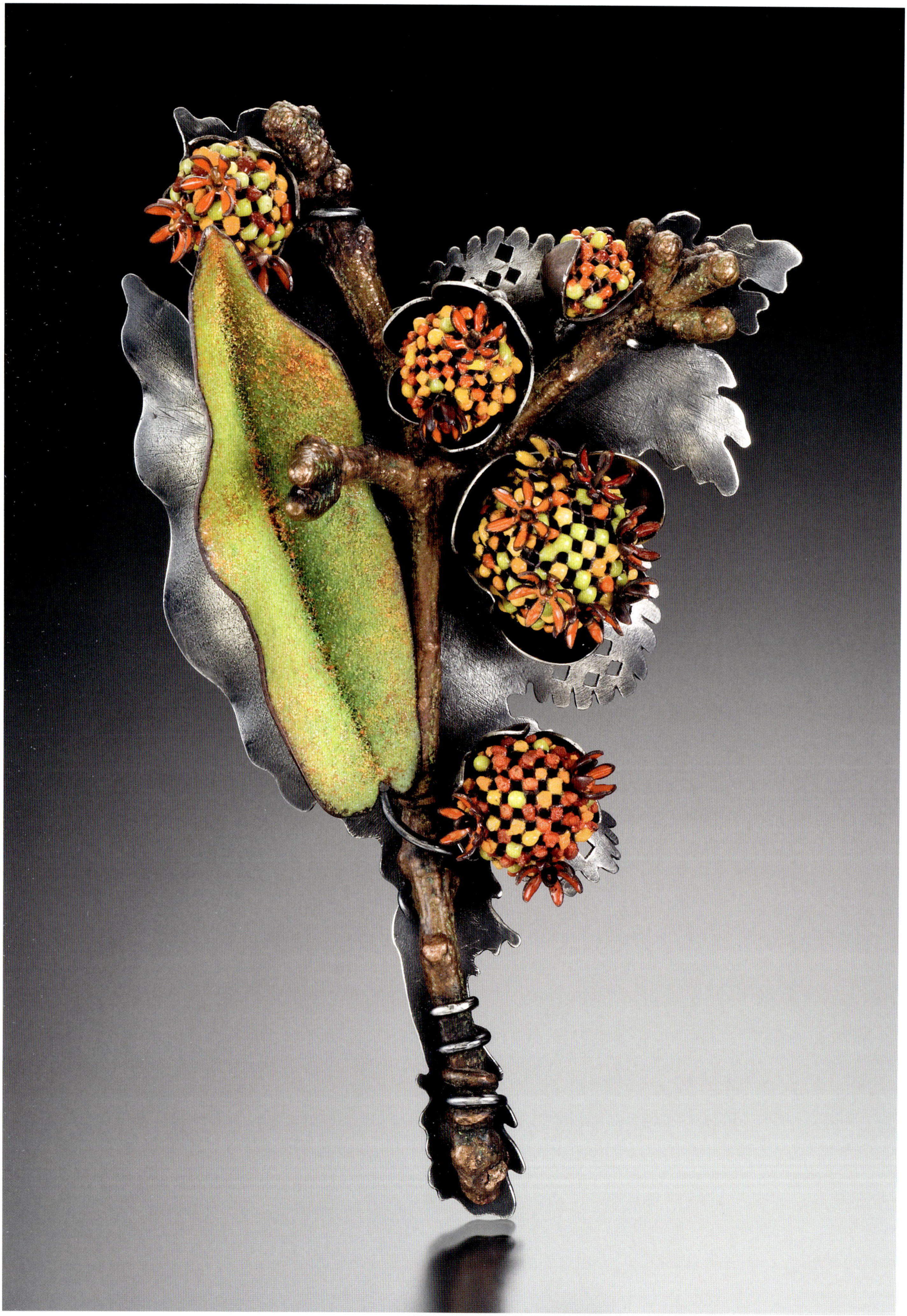

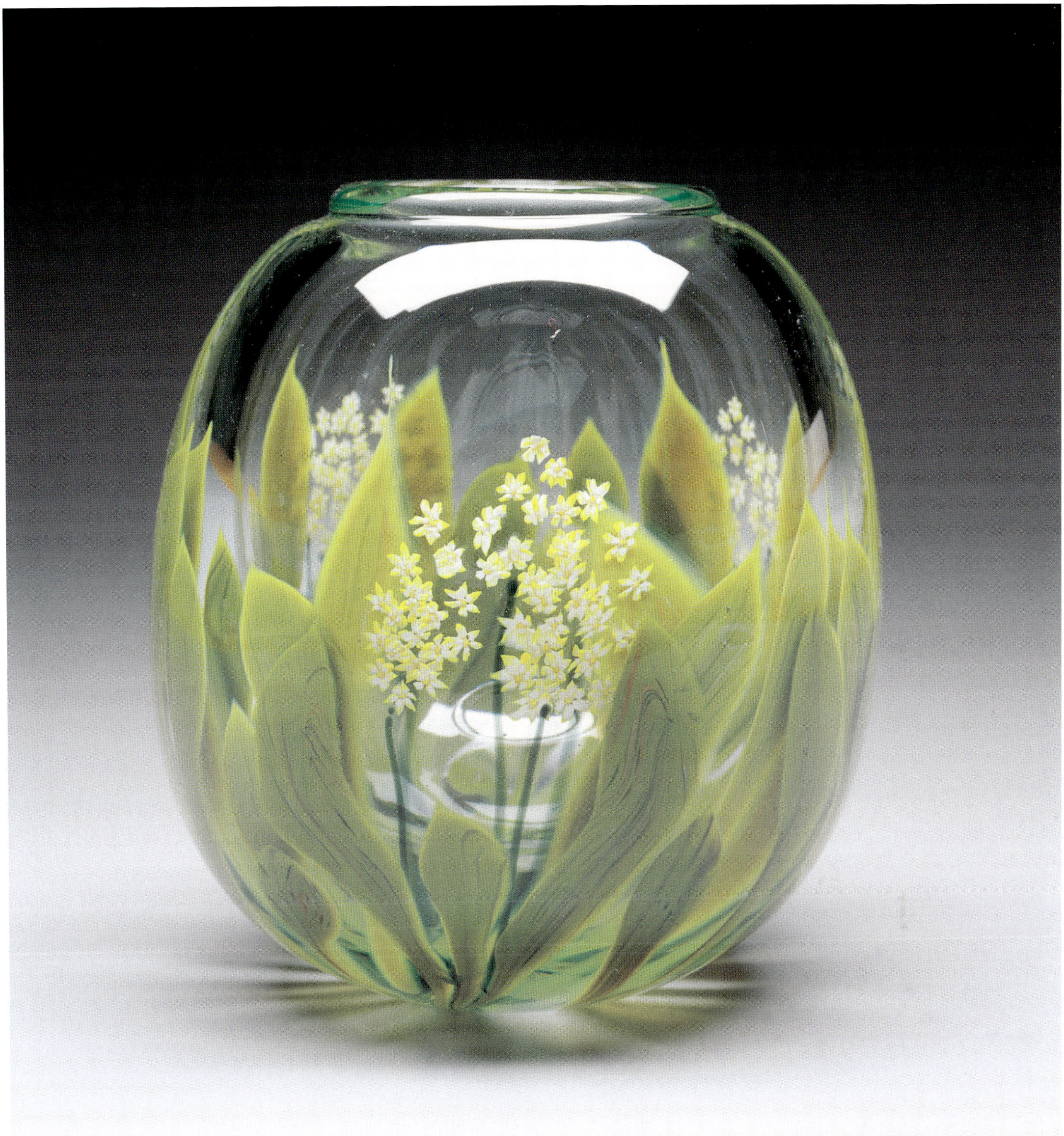

CAT. 35

Wendy McAllister (American, 1950–). *Grand Bois*, 2009, vitreous enamel, copper, sterling silver, Prismacolor pencil, 4.75" x 3" x 1.5".

Gift of Patty and Bill Gorelick. 2011.75
Photo: Hap Sakwa Photography

CAT. 36

Mark Peiser (American, 1938–). *Lilies of the Valley*, 1978, blown and lampworked glass, zinc crystal, 6.75" x 6.5".

Gift of Sonia and Isaac Luski. 1986.28.9.
© Mark C. Peiser 1978

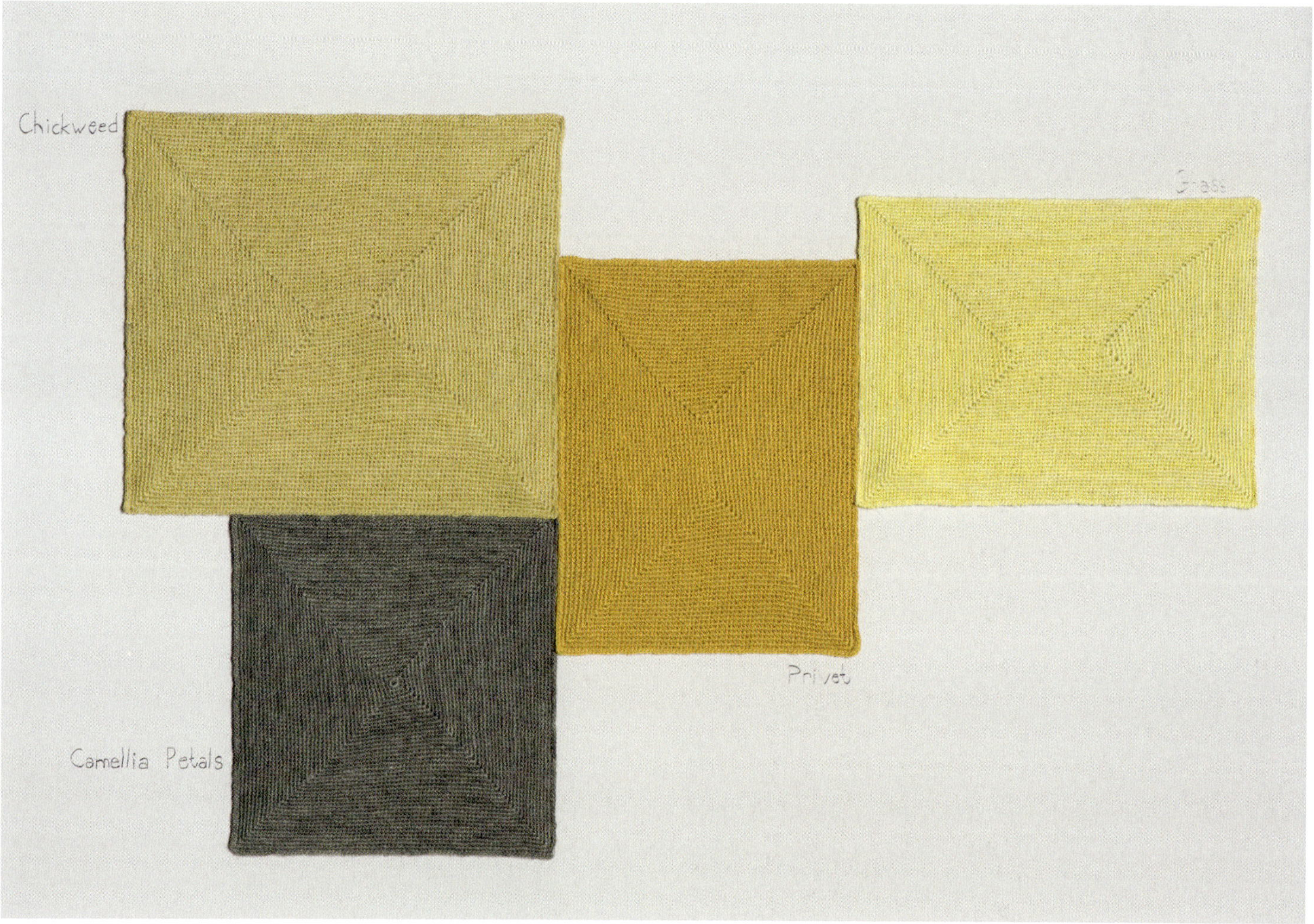

CAT. 37

Hildur Bjarnadóttir (Icelandic, 1969–). *Urban Color Palette, Charlotte* (detail), 2010, crocheted Icelandic wool, plant dyes, 103" x 148".

Project Ten Ten Ten Commission. Gift of Wesley Mancini, the International Textile Manufacturers Association, and Berhan Nebioglu and Michael Gallis, Michael Gallis and Associates. 2010.64A-KK. © Hildur Bjarnadóttir 2010
Photo: David H. Ramsey

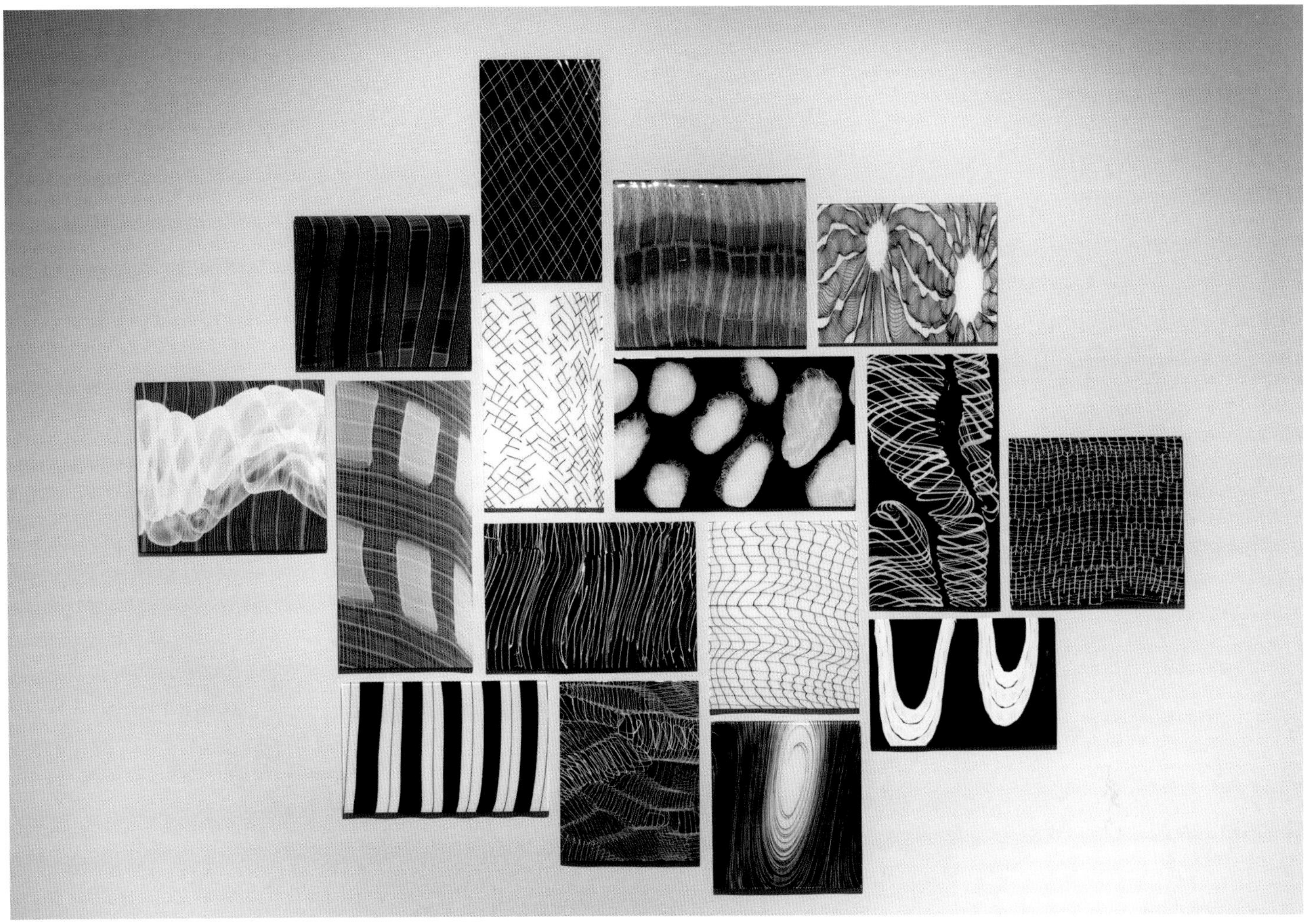

CAT. 38

Nancy Callan (American, 1964–).
***Spin, Weave, Gather*, 2018,**
blown and slumped glass ,
102.25" x 132.25" x 0 .875".

Gift of lead donors Lorne Lassiter and Gary Ferraro, Judy and John Alexander, Sandy Berlin, Linda and Bill Farthing, The Founders' Circle, Libba and Mike Gaither, William Gorelick, Barbara Loughlin, Jancy and Gilbert Patrick, Mark Ridenhour, Vicki Jones, Yvonne and Richard McCracken, Sara and Bob McDonnell, Britt and Greg Hill, and Deborah Halliday and Gary Rautenstrauch. 2019.8A-O
Photo: Brandon Scott

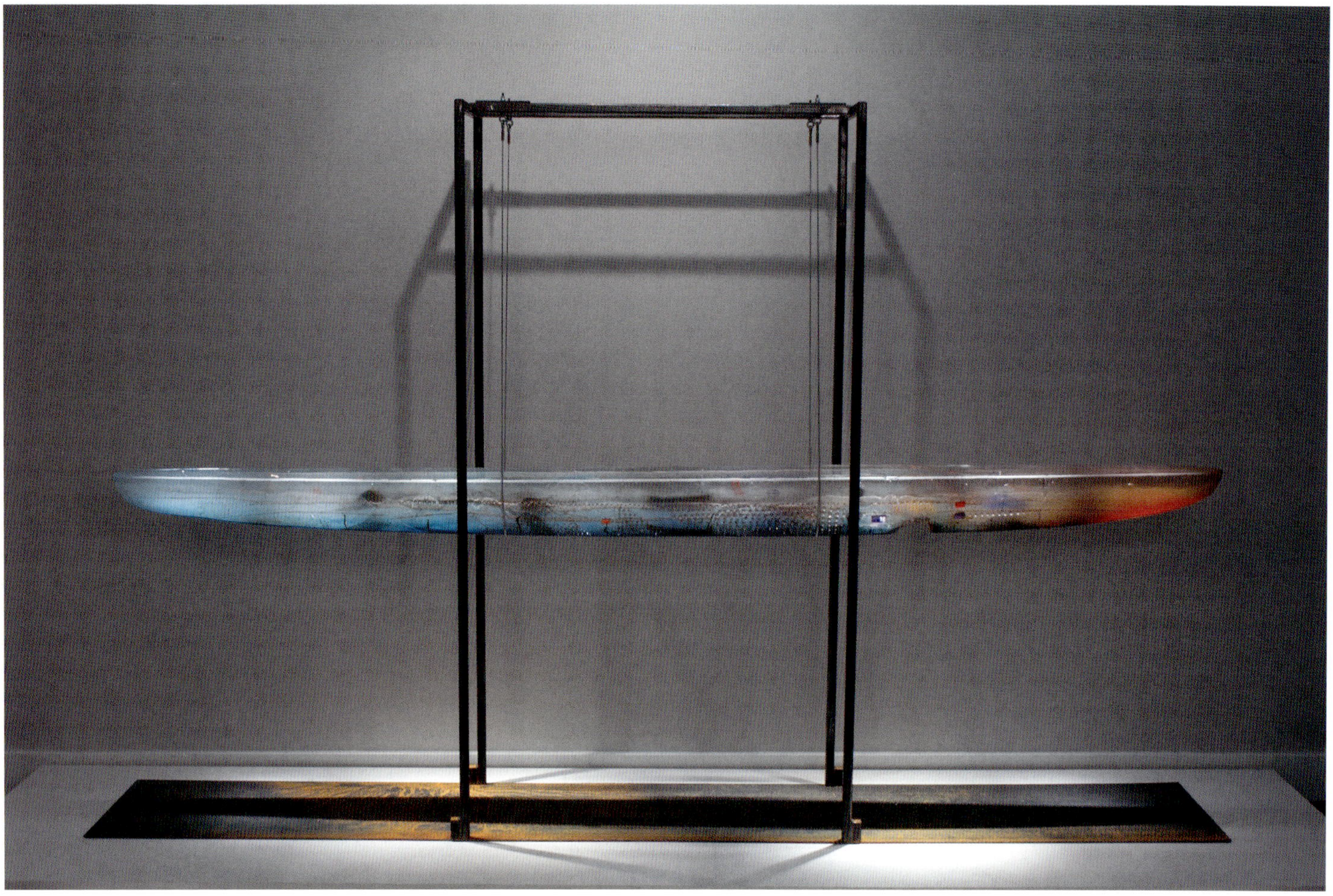

CAT. 39 (ABOVE AND OPPOSITE)
Bertil Vallien (Swedish, 1938–).
***King's Voyage*, 1996, sand-cast glass, copper, full lead crystal, 117" x 6" x 6".**
Gift of Lisa S. and Dudley B. Anderson in honor of Hugh McColl. 2002.120. © Bertil Vallien 1996
Photo: Brandon Scott

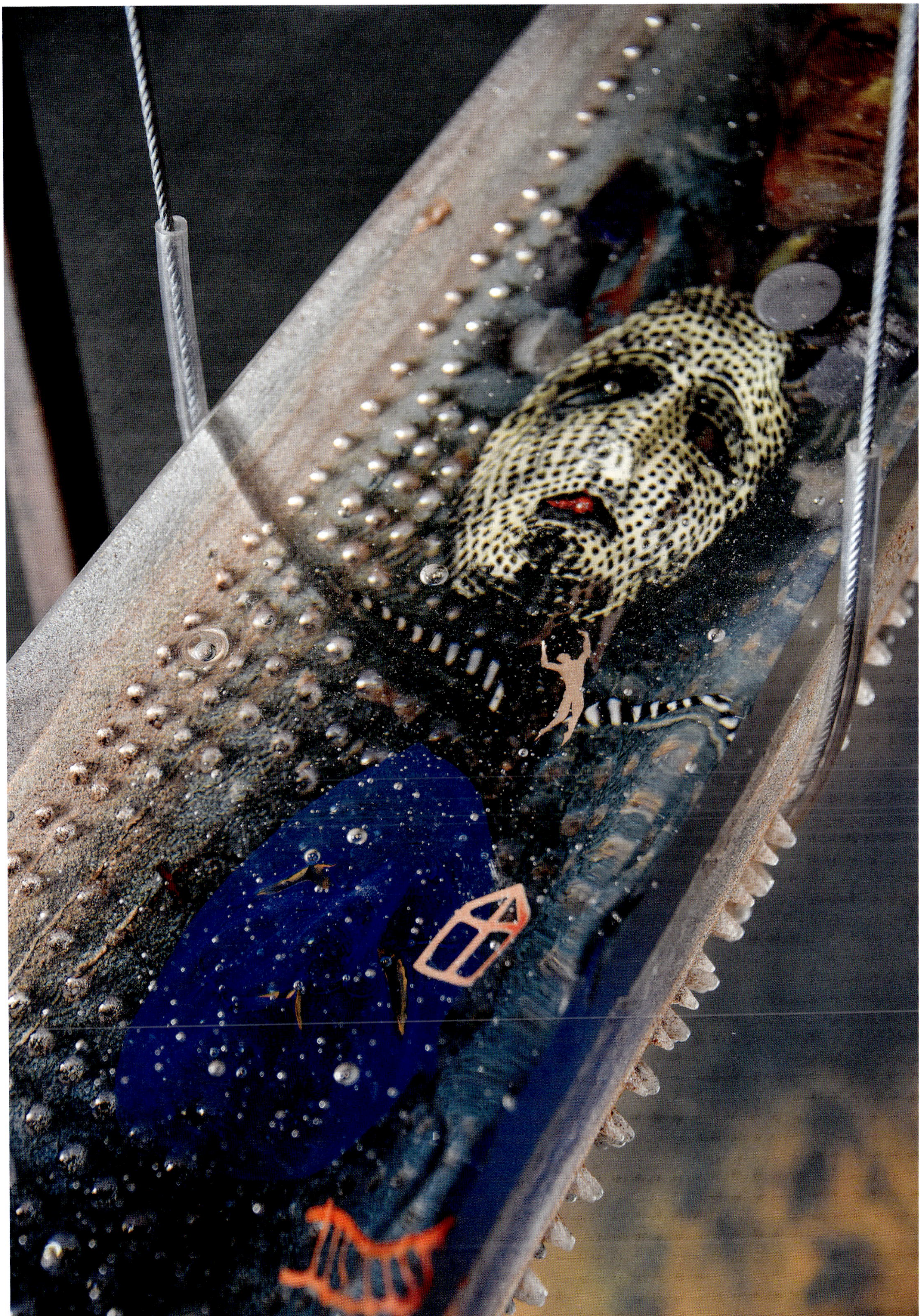

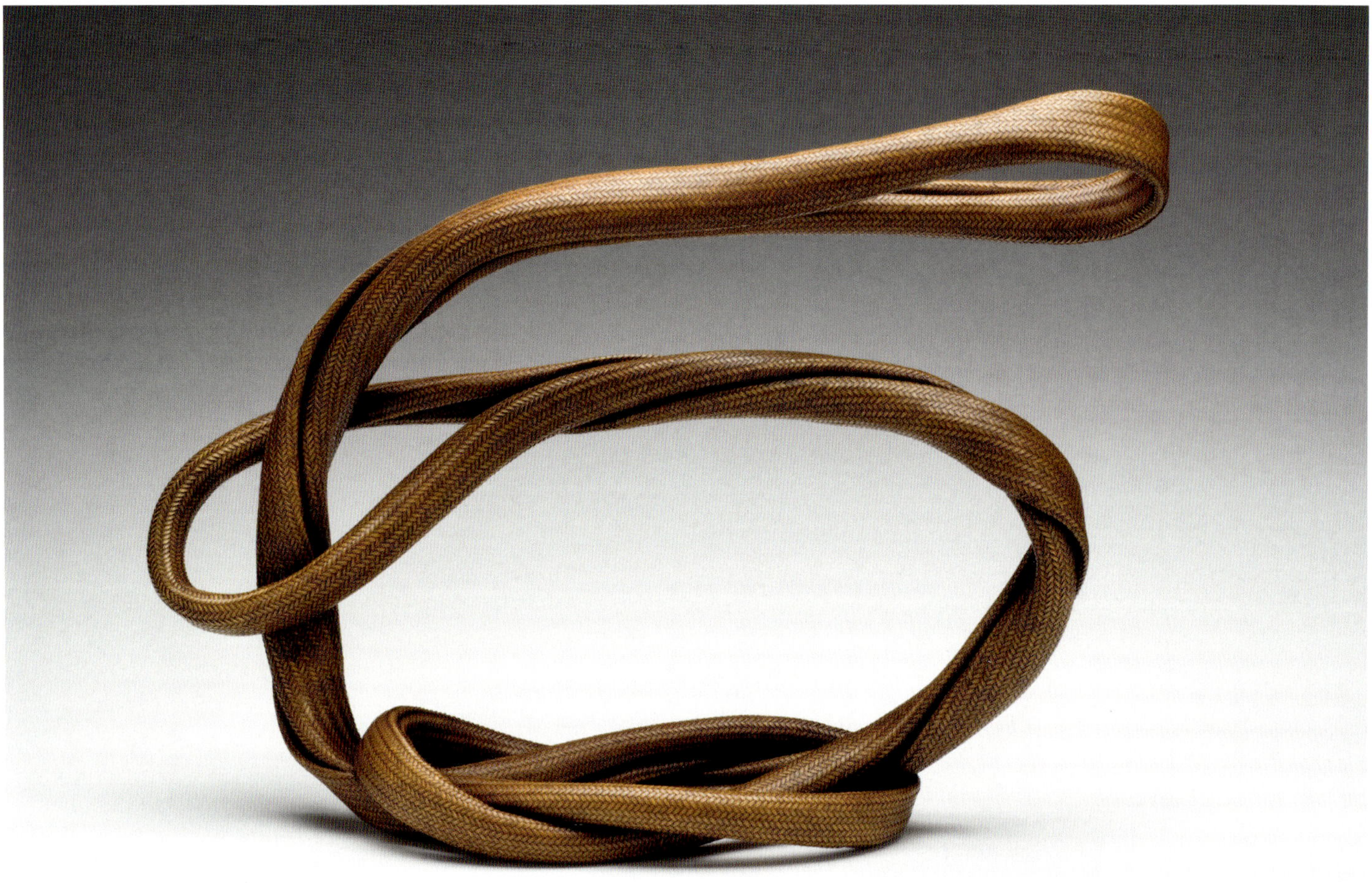

CAT. 40

Honda Syoryu (Japanese, 1951–). *Untitled*, 2005, twill-plated (ajiro-ami) and dyed madake bamboo, 22" x 6.5" x 16".

Museum Purchase: Funds provided by Ginger M. Kemp. 2007.61
Photo: David H. Ramsey

CAT. 41

Nicholas Arroyave-Portela (British, 1972–). *Slashed Piece*, 2002, earthenware, terra sigillata, 18.75" x 7.5".

Gift of Diane and Marc Grainer. 2016.1.3

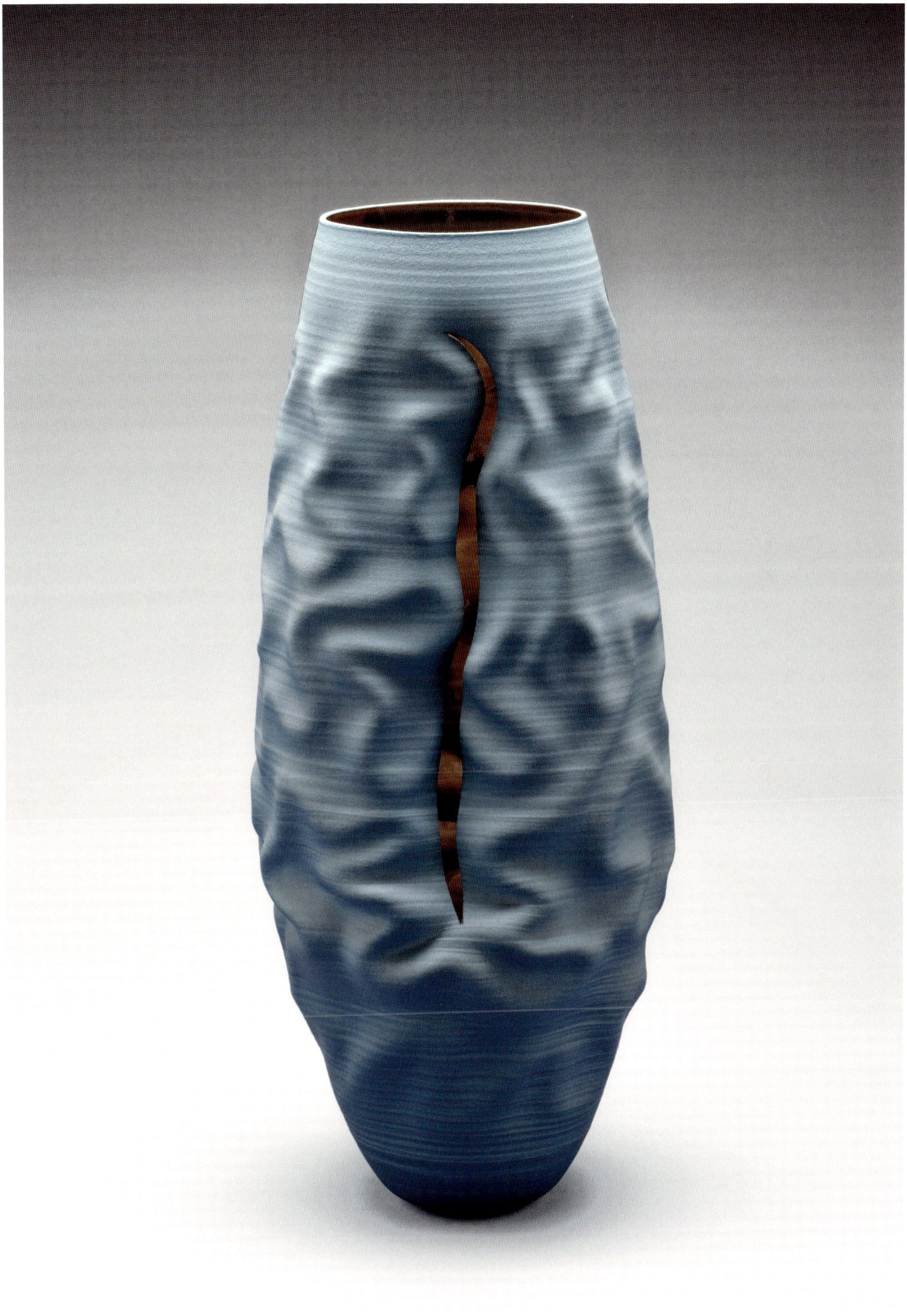

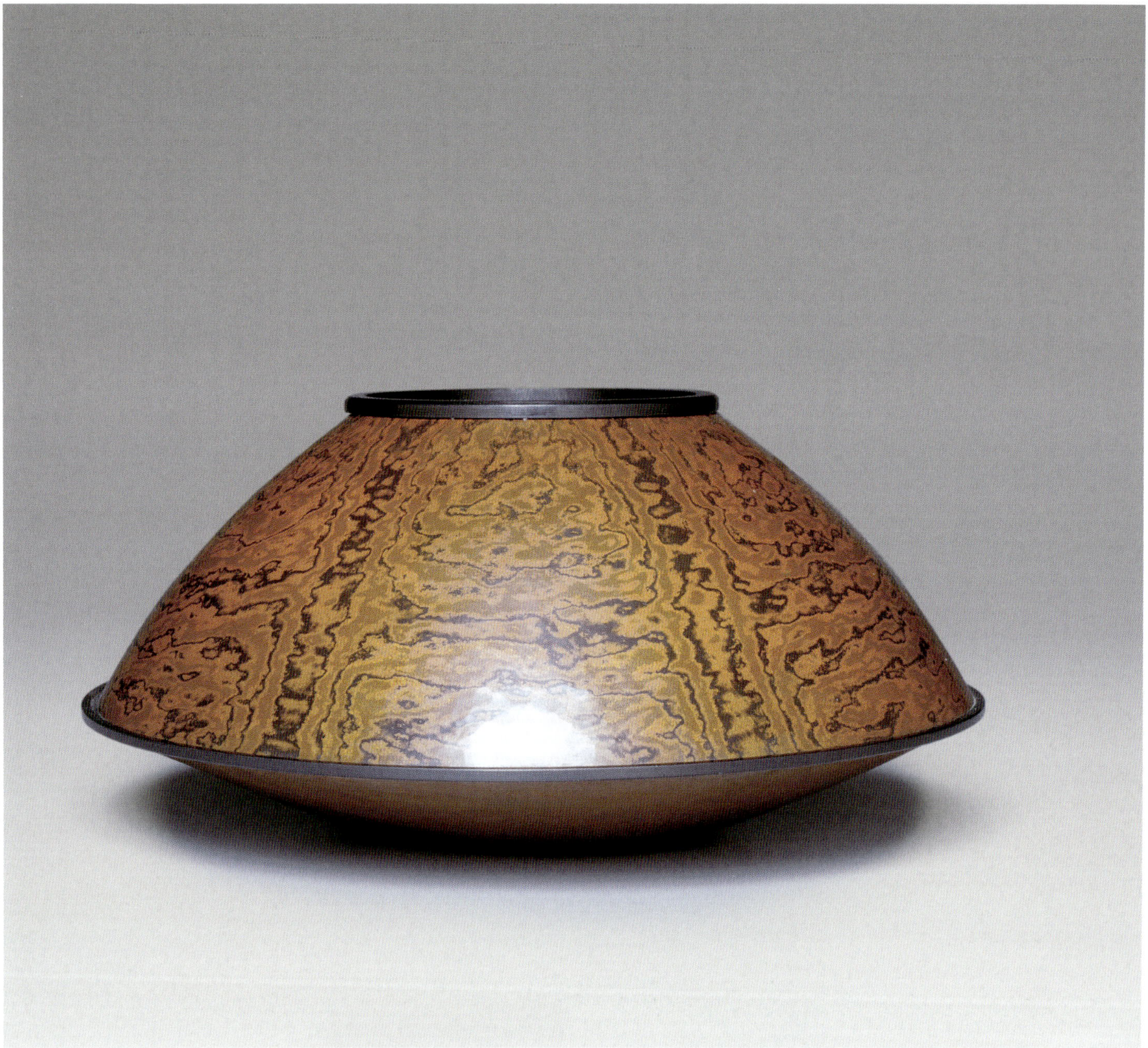

CAT. 42
Marvin Jensen (American, 1945–).
***Interior Structure*, 1991, forged and raised copper, shibuichi, kuromido, shakudo, anodized aluminum, 4.5" x 9.375".**
Gift of Mignon Durham. 1998.118

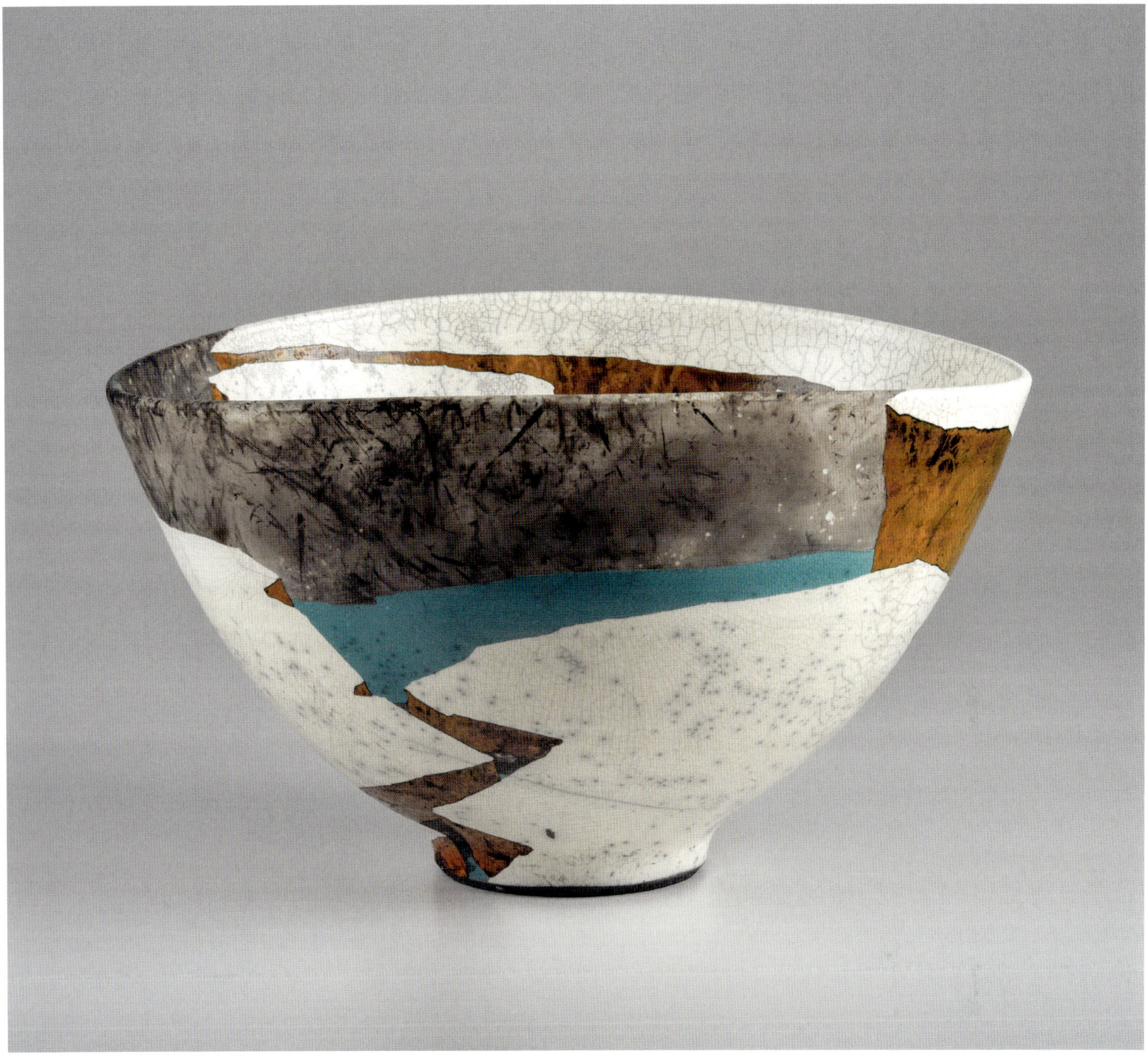

CAT. 43

Wayne Higby (American, 1943–).
***Sun Rim Canyon*, 1984, wheel-thrown and raku-fired earthenware, slip, glaze, 10.375" x 18.25" x 15.625".**

Allan Chasanoff Ceramic Collection.
2003.91.14. © Wayne Higby 1984
Photo: Brandon Scott

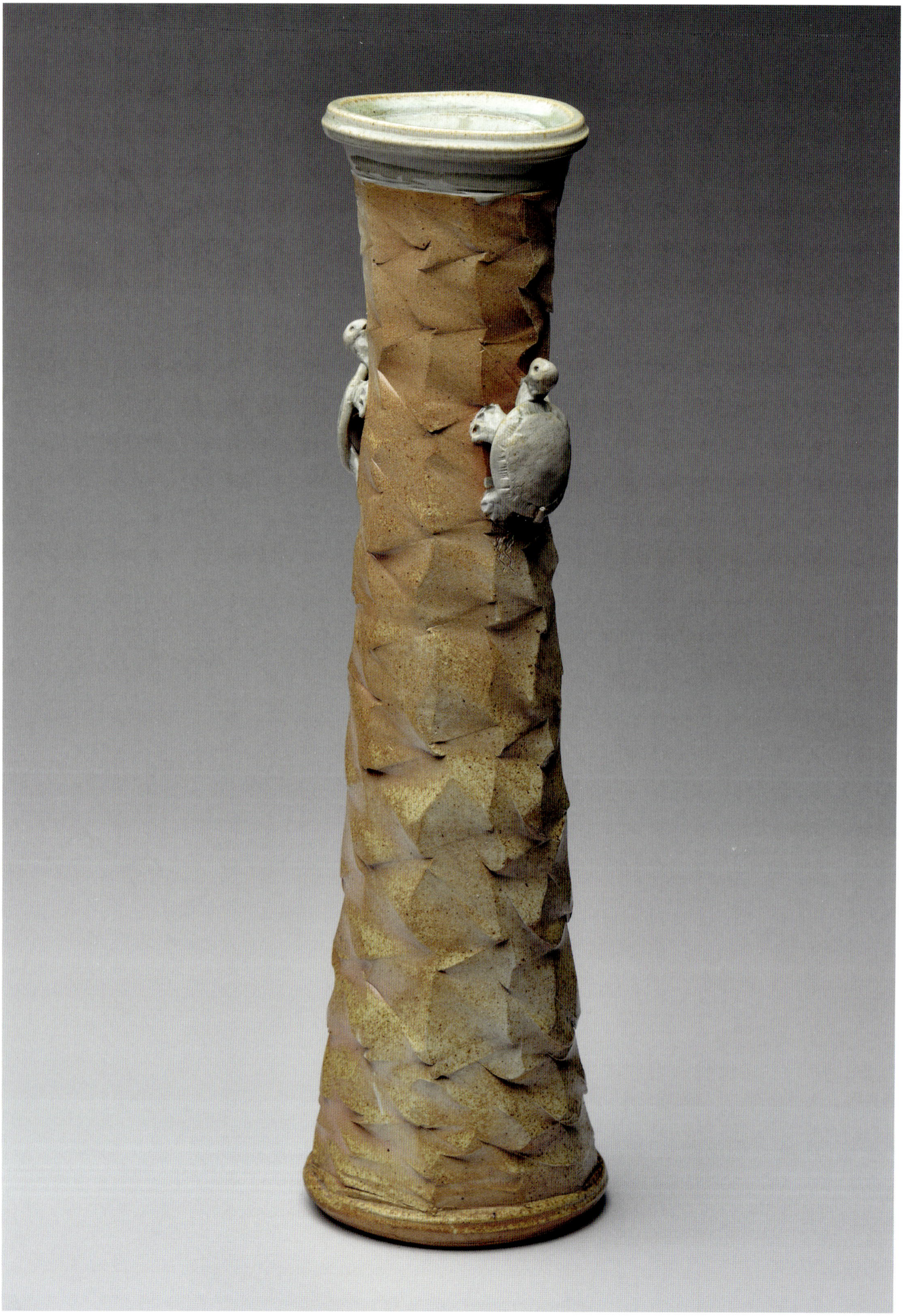

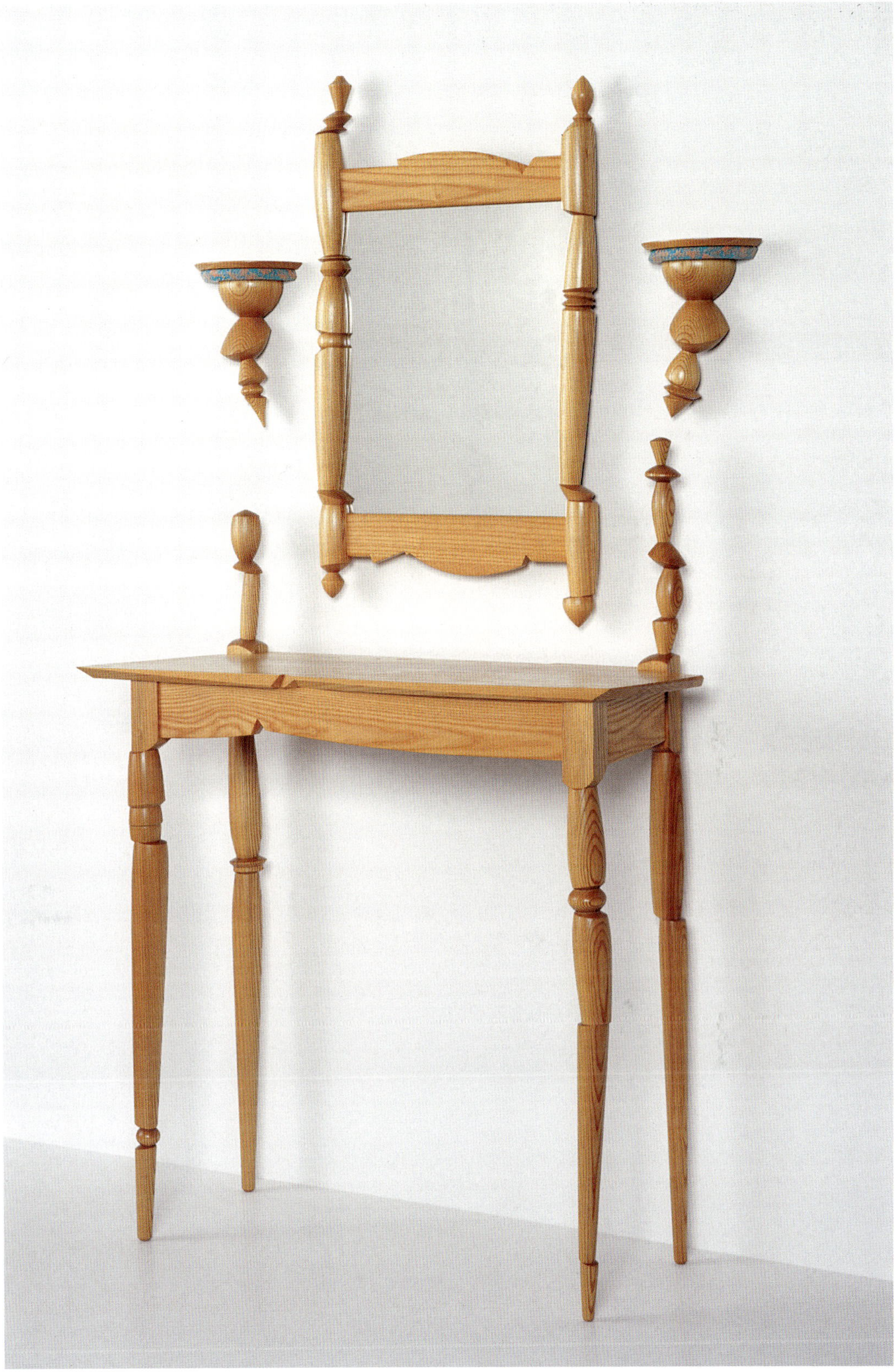

CAT. 44

Cynthia Bringle (American, 1939–).
***Turtle Vase*, circa 2004–5, wheel-thrown, carved, wood-fired, and salt-fired stoneware, 24" x 6.5" x 5.5".**
Gift of Ann and Tom Cousins. 2005.77.2
Photo: Brandon Scott

CAT. 45

Mark Sfirri (American, 1952–).
***Furniture Set*, 1993, turned ash wood, mirror, paint, 80" x 46" x 18.5".**
Museum Purchase: Funds provided by John and Robyn Horn. 1998.29.1-3

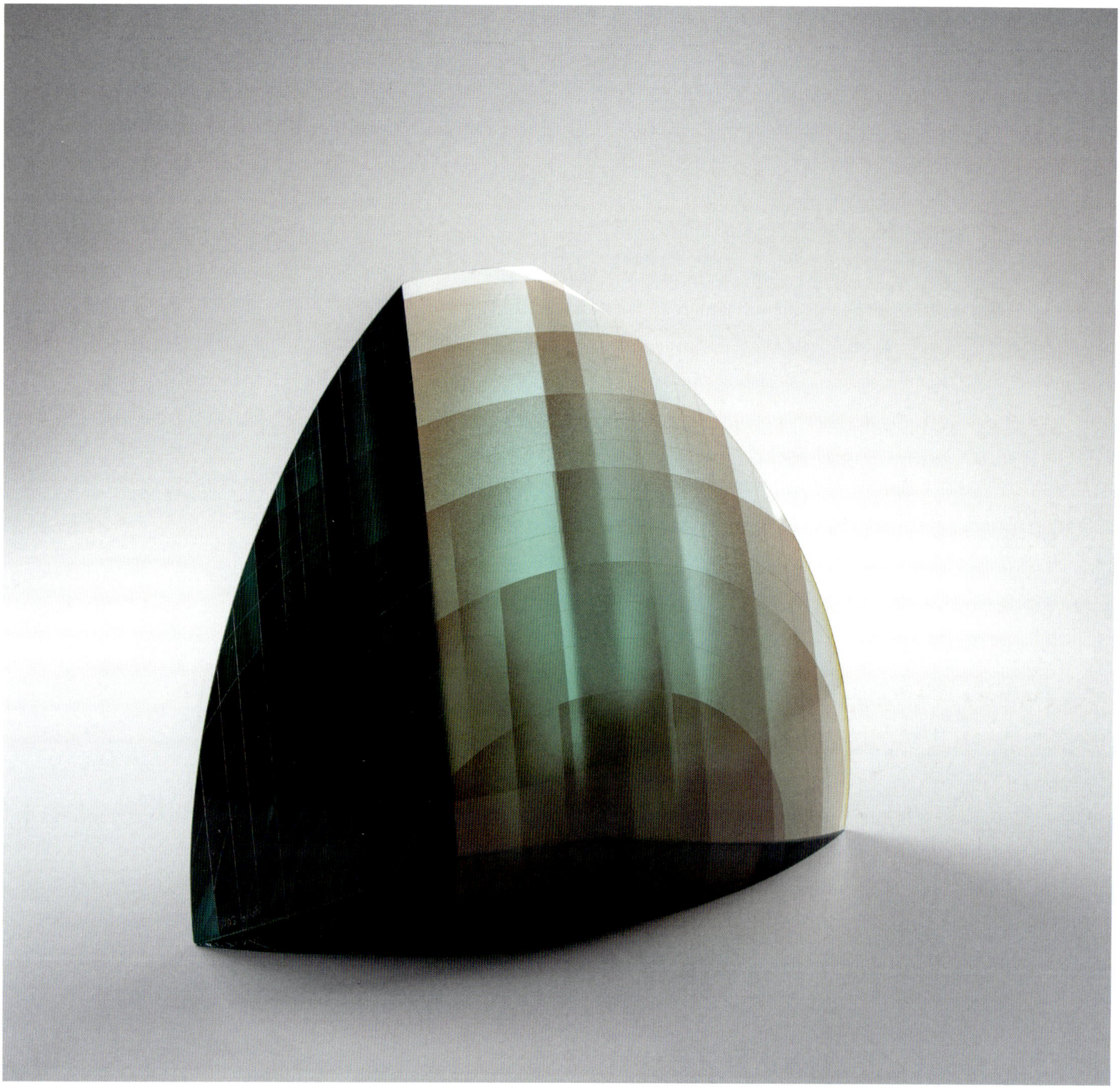

CAT. 46

Zoltán Bohus (Hungarian, 1941–2017).
***Stratofera*, 2002, laminated glass,**
12.75" x 16" x 6.625".
Gift of Lorne Lassiter and Gary Ferraro. 2017.5.5
Photo: Brandon Scott

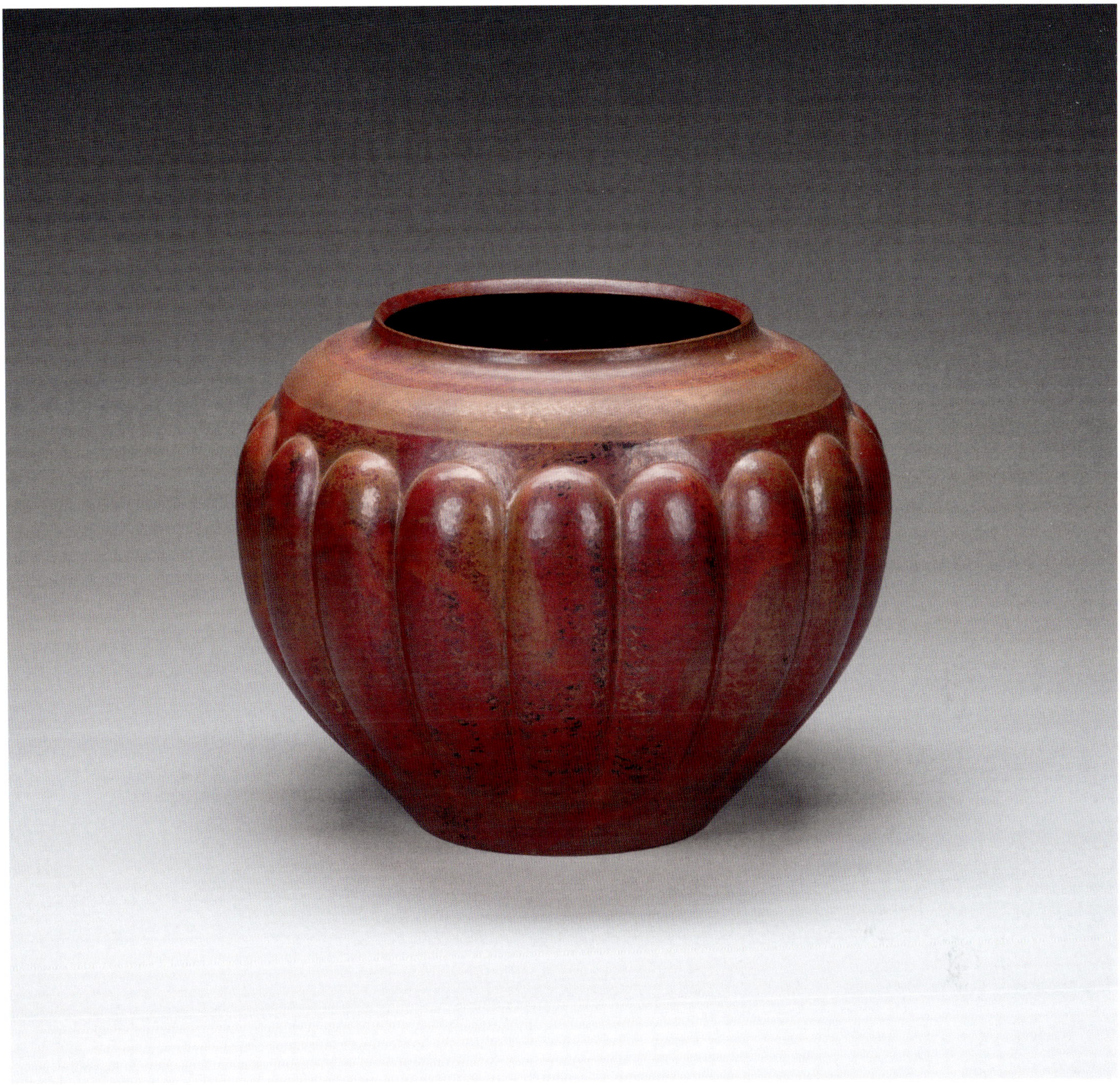

CAT. 47

Etelberto Ramirez Tinoco (Mexican, 1944–1993). *Vessel*, 20th century, copper, 10.875" x 13".

Gift of Gretchen and Nelson Grice. 2016.36.258

Photo: Brandon Scott

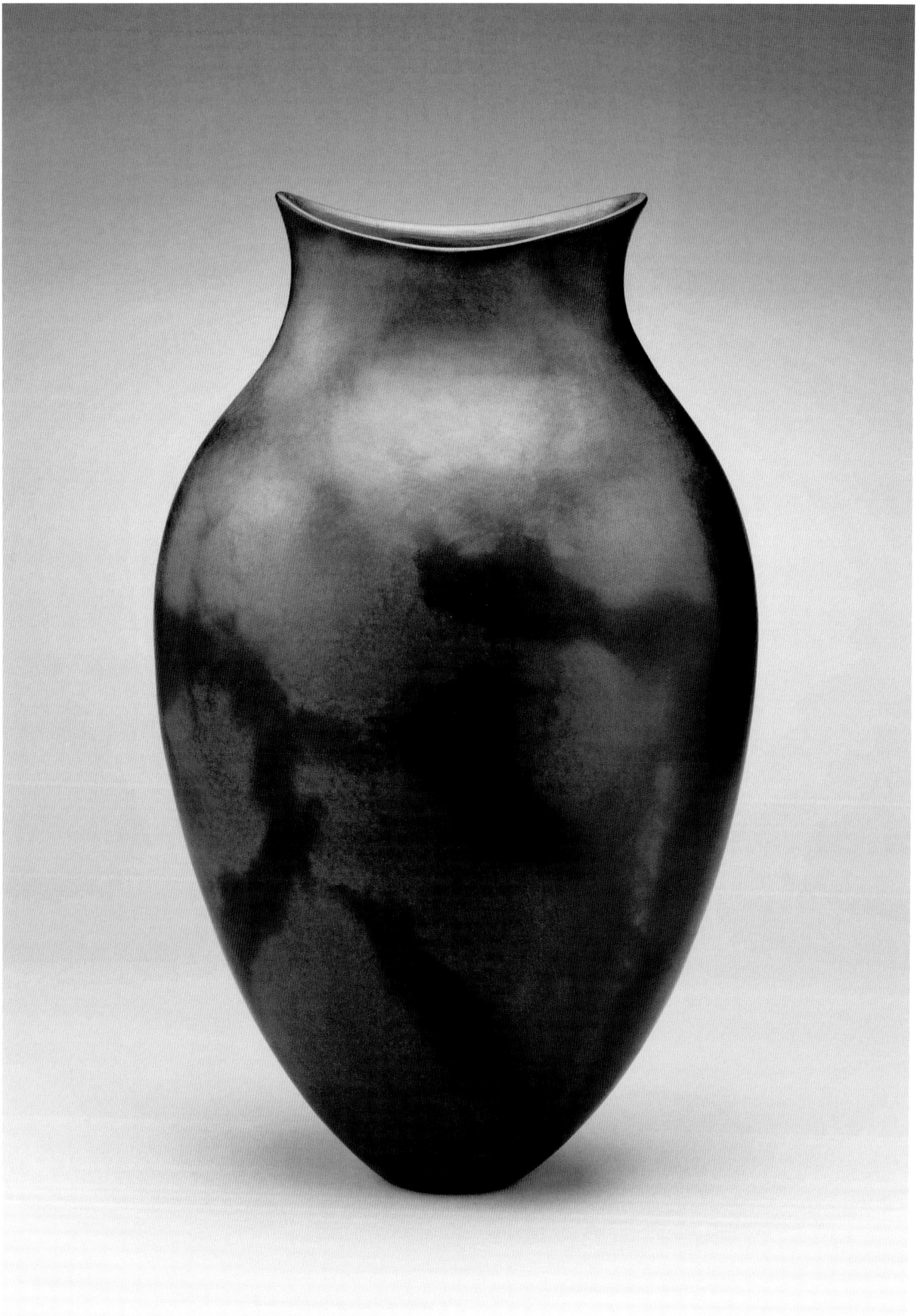

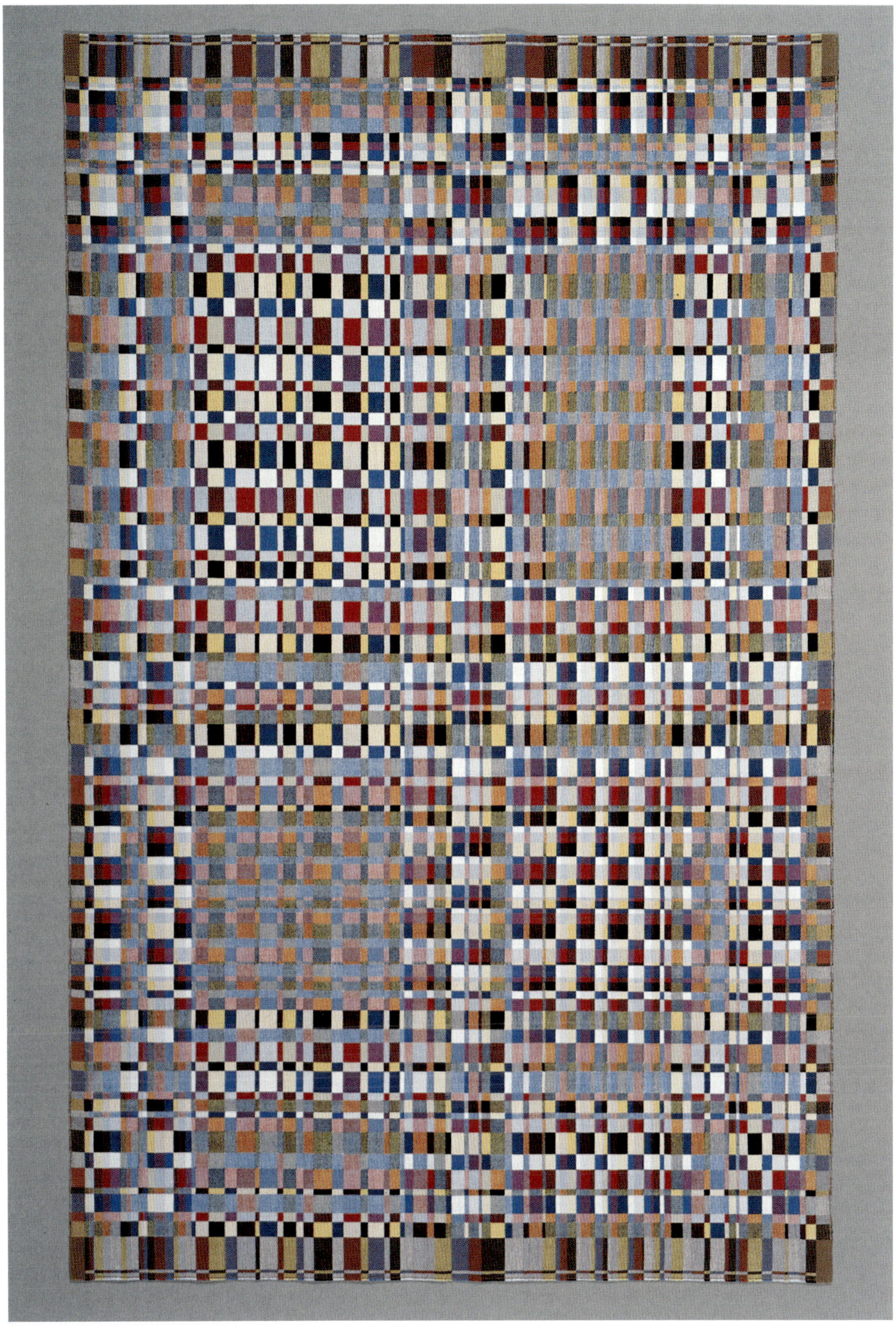

CAT. 48

Gabriele Koch (German, 1948–).
Flattened Tall Form, 1993, coil-built, burnished, and smoke-fired T-material, slip, 16.5" x 10" x 3.5".

Gift of Diane and Marc Grainer. 2011.36.20

CAT. 49

Richard Landis (American, 1931–).
Computer Series – Untitled, circa 1980, double-woven mercerized cotton, 21" x 33".

Gift of James and Joanne Rapp. 1999.105.

ACKNOWLEDGMENTS

Annie Carlano
Rebecca E.Elliot

The creation of *Craft in the Laboratory: The Science of Making Things* involved many individuals. First and foremost, we thank the artists whose works piqued our curiosity and spurred us to investigate. Beyond those whose work is depicted and discussed in this book, there are others whose work is included in the Craft + Design galleries; we are grateful to them all.

Natalie Frazier Allen, Chair, Board of Trustees, and Sean Jones, Past Chair, Board of Trustees, have our gratitude. Gifted colleagues at the Mint Museum contributed their expertise to the exhibition. In particular, we thank Todd A. Herman, PhD, President & CEO; Jen Sudul Edwards, Chief Curator & Curator of Contemporary Art; Michele Leopold, Director of Collections & Exhibitions, and the entire Collections & Exhibitions team; Rebecca O'Malley, Exhibitions Coordinator; Katherine Steiner, Chief Registrar; HannaH Crowell, Head of Exhibition Design; Hailey D. Bryer, Exhibitions Graphic Designer; Ian Larson, Chief of Art Services & Installation; Mitch Francis and Jeff Crawford, Art Services & Installation technicians; Cynthia Moreno, Director of Learning & Engagement; Gennifer Stanley, former Assistant Head of School & Gallery Programs; Rubie Britt-Height, Director of Community Relations; Hillary Cooper, Director of Advancement; Katie Miller, Director of Development; Martha Snell, Grants & Advancement Coordinator; Caroline Portillo, Director of Marketing & Communications; Thesha Woodley, Associate Director of Visitor Experience & Membership; and Amy Smith Grigg, Manager & Buyer for Retail Operations.

Originating content, compiling images, editing, working on layout, and producing an art book requires a range of specialized talent. At the Mint, Rebecca Merriman handled image rights and coordinated sessions with Brandon Scott, contract photographer. Joyce Weaver, Director of Library & Archives, handled many inter-library loan and new book orders. Joel Smeltzer, Head of School & Gallery Programs, added visual punch and his own inquisitiveness for the twenty-first-century reader. At D Giles Limited, Dan Giles was immediately drawn to the topic of this book and cheerfully accommodated our occasional deviations from "the plan." At Giles we also thank Allison McCormick, Editorial Manager, as well as Louise Parfitt, Ocky Murray, Louise Ramsay, and Harry Ault. It was a pleasure working through the many details of this book with such a talented team.

Annie Carlano extends much gratitude to Avery Close, postgraduate researcher (volunteer), and to the following for over a decade of studio visits and ongoing conversations about their craft: Kate Malone, Danny Lane, Tom Joyce, Cristina Córdova, Ben Owen III, Joseph Walsh, and Laura Kishimoto. For facilitating research, Eugenie and Lael Johnson, John Palmer, Larry Brady, Ann and Michael Tarwater, Beth Quartapella, Lauren Harkey, Sarah Myerscough, and Adrian Sassoon. Most of all, I thank Rebecca Elliot for coming up with what is not only a brilliant exhibition topic, but is ever timely, as the COVID-19 world has witnessed the interconnectedness of artists/designers and scientists who are working collaboratively to manage a horrific pandemic. Her impeccable research skills, thoroughness, and enthusiasm for the science of craft and design make this a project of excellence.

Rebecca Elliot thanks Annie Carlano for her recognition and support of this important and rewarding project. She also thanks Joel Smeltzer and Gennifer Stanley as well as evaluation consultant Mary Beth Ausman for their collaborative work. Thanks go to the four teams of art and science/math teacher participants in the museum's first-ever Teacher Fellowship: Meghan Bechtold and Rupi Young; Brandt Boidy and Jackie Royce; Jennifer Ford and Lisa Snead; and Abbie Hess and Kristen Ward.

Research travel was essential to this project. Thank you to the artists who welcomed us into their studios: Elizabeth Brim, Cynthia Bringle, David Ellsworth, Donald Fortescue, Chad Alice Hagen, Hoss Haley, Marvin Jensen, Ben Owen III, and Mark Peiser. Thanks also to Kathryn Gremley of the Penland School of Craft for facilitating our visits to nearby artists. We are deeply grateful to the many other individuals who met with us and lent their expertise: Hsien-Yi Chien, Dr. Joshua Gutwill, Meghan Kroning, Dr. Jessica Parker, and Karen Wilkinson (The Exploratorium, San Francisco); Takuro Shibata (STARworks, Star, North Carolina); Jackson Martin, Jeannie Regan, Leslie Rowenberg, Sara Sanders, Brent Skidmore, Justin Turcotte, and Matthew West (the STEAM Studio, University of North Carolina Asheville); and Charla Fields (Discovery Place, Charlotte, NC).

Louis Foreman and his team at Enventys lent their knowledge and expertise to early conversations about the production of the installation's interactives.

Catalogue contributors Zoe Laughlin, co-founder/director of the Institute of Making and the Materials Library project, University College London, and Hideo Mabuchi, Professor of Applied Physics, Stanford University and head of the Mabuchi Lab, are artists, as well as engineer and physicist who apply the same methodology to both spheres of their activities with exceptional results; this made them ideal co-authors. Their fine writing and passion for their blended professional lives is palpable.

This book was published to coincide with the re-installation of the Mint Museum's permanent galleries of Craft and Design.

12th February, 2022 – ongoing

Mint Museum Uptown at Levine Center for the Arts
500 South Tryon Street
Charlotte, North Carolina 28202
www.mintmuseum.org

First published in 2022 by GILES
An imprint of D Giles Limited
66 High Street
Lewes, BN7 1XG, UK
gilesltd.com

ISBN (hardcover): 978-1-911282-72-3

Craft in the Laboratory: The Science of Making Things is presented with support from the National Endowment for the Arts.

The Mint Museum is funded, in part, with operating support from the Arts & Science Council of Charlotte-Mecklenburg, Inc.; the North Carolina Arts Council, a division of the Department of Cultural Resources; the City of Charlotte; and its members.

The Mint Museum is supported, in part, by the Infusion Fund and its generous donors.

Library of Congress Cataloging-in-Publication Data

Names: Mint Museum (Charlotte, N.C.), author. | Elliot, Rebecca (Rebecca E.) | Carlano, Annie. | Laughlin, Zoe, 1981- | Mabuchi, Hideo. | Smeltzer, Joel.
Title: Craft in the laboratory : the science of making things / Rebecca E. Elliot, Annie Carlano, Zoe Laughlin, Hideo Mabuchi, Joel Smeltzer.
Description: Charlotte, North Carolina : The Mint Museum in association with D. Giles Limited, [2022] | Includes bibliographical references. | Summary: "This book was published in conjunction with the exhibition Craft in the Laboratory: The Science of Making Things, organized by the Mint Museum, Charlotte, North Carolina"-- Provided by publisher.
Identifiers: LCCN 2021023901 | ISBN 9781911282723 (hardcover)
Subjects: LCSH: Handicraft--Technique. | Handicraft--North Carolina--Charlotte. | Decorative arts--Technique. | Creation (Literary, artistic, etc.) | Science--Methodology. | Art and science. | Decorative arts--North Carolina--Charlotte. | Mint Museum (Charlotte, N.C.)
Classification: LCC TT23 .M56 2022 | DDC 680--dc23
LC record available at https://lccn.loc.gov/2021023901

For D Giles Limited:
Copy-edited and proofread by Sarah Kane
Designed by Ocky Murray
Produced by GILES, an imprint of D Giles Limited
Reprographics by Bredero Graphics, Belgium
Printed by Albe de Coker, Belgium

All measurements are in inches and centimeters and are indicated in height by width by depth.

Front cover: Danny Lane (American, 1955–). *Threshold* (detail), 2010, stacked plate glass, molded glass, and steel. Project Ten Ten Ten Commission. Museum Purchase: Exchange funds from various donors; Gift of William and Patty Gorelick, Drew and Beth Quartapella, Shelton and Carol Gorelick, John and Stacy Sumner Jesso, Richard and Yvonne McCracken, and the Founders' Circle Cause 2009 contributors. 2010.70.

All images courtesy The Mint Museum unless otherwise noted.

Front cover: detail of cat. 8 (pp. 44–45)
pp. 2–3: detail of cat. 33 (p. 76)
p. 4: detail of cat. 14 (p. 52)
p. 6: detail of cat. 13 (p. 51)
p. 8: detail of cat. 21 (p. 63)
p. 12: detail of cat. 7 (p. 43)
p. 14: detail of cat. 3 (p. 38)
p. 18: detail of cat. 31 (p. 75)
p. 30: detail of cat. 16 (p. 58)
pp. 32–33: detail of cat. 40 (p. 84)